Kaleidoscope

NCTE Bibliography Series

Kaleidoscope

A Multicultural Booklist for Grades K–8

Fourth Edition

**Nancy Hansen-Krening, Elaine M. Aoki,
and Donald T. Mizokawa, Editors**

and the Committee to Revise the Multicultural Booklist
of the National Council of Teachers of English

National Council of Teachers of English
1111 W. Kenyon Road, Urbana, IL 61801-1096

Staff Editor: Bonny Graham
Interior Design: Doug Burnett
Cover Design: Tom Jaczak
Series Cover Design: R. Maul

Cover illustration by Hermès Alègrè from "The Mats" written by Francisco Arcellana. Kane/Miller Book Publishers, 1999. © 1995 by Hermès Alègrè. Reprinted by permission.

NCTE Stock Number: 25395-3050

ISSN: 1051-4740

ISBN: 0-8141-2539-5

We dedicate this book with our love to Jared and Emma, Stacey and Jana, and Emily. These young people who are our grandchildren and our children represent the hope we hold for all children and youth.

About the NCTE Bibliography Series

The National Council of Teachers of English is proud to be part of a tradition that we want to share with you. In our bibliography series are four different booklists, each focused on a particular audience, each updated regularly. These are *Adventuring with Books* (pre–K through grade 6), *Kaleidoscope* (multicultural literature, grades K through 8), *Your Reading* (middle school/junior high), and *Books for You* (senior high). Together, these volumes list thousands of recent children's and young adult trade books. Although the works included cover a wide range of topics, they all have one thing in common: they're good books that students and teachers alike enjoy.

How are these volumes put together? The process begins when an educator who knows literature and its importance in the lives of students and teachers is chosen by the NCTE Executive Committee to serve as booklist editor. That editor then works with teachers and librarians who review, select, and annotate hundreds of new trade books sent to them by publishers. It's a complicated process, one that can last three or four years. But because of their dedication and strong belief in the need to let others know about the good literature that's available, these professionals volunteer their time in a way that is commendable and serves as an inspiration to all of us. The members of the committee that compiled this volume are listed in the front of the book, and we are truly grateful for their hard work.

As educators know, no single book is right for every reader or every purpose, so inclusion in this booklist is not necessarily an endorsement from NCTE. But it does indicate that the professionals who make up the booklist committee feel that the work in question is worthy of teachers' and students' attention, whether for its informative or aesthetic qualities. Similarly, exclusion from an NCTE booklist is not necessarily a judgment on the quality of a given book or publisher. Many factors—space, time, availability of certain books, publisher participation—may influence the final shape of the list.

We hope that you'll find this booklist a useful resource in discovering new titles and authors, and we hope that you will want to collect other booklists in the series. Our mission is to help improve the teaching and learning of English and the language arts, and we hope you'll agree that the quality of our booklists contributes substantially toward that goal.

Zarina M. Hock
Senior Editor

Contents

Acknowledgments

Before our committee completed this edition of *Kaleidoscope*, we learned that it was to be the final edition. It was sobering news because we all agree that the need for this special book remains. When Phillip Lee, publisher of Lee & Low Books, told us that the number of books published by authors of color is decreasing, we realized that the need for visible, strong support for these books remains. Our acknowledgments have assumed a now greater importance.

We gratefully acknowledge:

- Rudine Sims Bishop, who began this series and continues to fight the good fight
- The remarkable authors of color who persevere in telling their stories
- The illustrators who illuminate our worlds
- The publishing companies who sent us the books of many of these authors and illustrators
- Jerry Purcell, who had the onerous task not only of organizing all the books we received but also preparing the initial drafts of the numbered annotations
- Allen Glenn, Dean, College of Education; Francis Hunkins, Area Chairman, Curriculum and Instruction; and Claudine Trafford, Area Administrator, at the University of Washington, Seattle, who offered continuing support
- The editors of previous editions of *Kaleidoscope*
- Pete Feely and Kurt Austin, NCTE editors, who provided strong support and encouragement throughout our work

Introduction

Nancy Hansen-Krening, Donald T. Mizokawa,
and Elaine M. Aoki

The fourth edition of *Kaleidoscope* continues the tradition of focusing on stories by and about people of color living in the United States. Specifically, the book provides an annotated bibliography of books published from 1999 to 2001 featuring protagonists who are Native American, African American, Asian American, or Latino American.

A weakness of categorizing by ethnic group is that it ignores the fact that categorizing a book as African American, for example, indicates nothing about whether the author writes from the perspective of a recent immigrant from Ethiopia or from the perspective of one who traces his or her roots back to eighteenth-century America. Furthermore, these designations lump different cultures together. Asian American literature, for instance, broadly includes stories about folks who might trace their roots to countries such as India, Cambodia, Uzbekistan, Japan, Korea, or the Philippine Islands.

This phenomenon clouds research data, too. Statistical profiles can show European Americans and Asian Americans to be distinctly different. On the other hand, when disaggregated, the profiles of Korean Americans, Japanese Americans, Filipino Americans, Vietnamese Americans, and Chinese Americans are not only distinct from one another and from European Americans, but they are different from aggregate Asian Americans as well (Mizokawa & Ryckman, 1990; Mizokawa, 1992). The blind spots created by lumping apply also to African Americans, Native Americans, Latinos, European Americans, and others.

The *Kaleidoscope* series was first edited by Rudine Sims Bishop (1994). In that book, she gave visibility to groups whose stories and faces were missing from too many libraries and classrooms; that edition was preceded by her book *Shadow and Substance* (1982), in which she wrote:

> There has been progress in the efforts to desegregate the world of children's books. We are *not* where we want to be, since gentle doses of racism are still being offered through children's books. But with cautious optimism we can report that we are also *not* where we were. (p. 108; author's italics)

Clearly, in the past twenty years we have continued to make progress. Just as clearly, we are still not where we both need and want to be. People of color still struggle with invisibility in the canon emphasized by many schools and libraries. Still, we are *not* where we were. A few publishing companies such as Lee & Low are dedicated to publishing stories about children of color. At every NCTE and IRA conference there are presentations on literature by and about people of color. However isolated these instances of dedication to visibility and equity for all might be, they do exist. If we are ever to learn about perspectives other than our own, if we are ever to have empathy for one another, we must hear the voices and see the faces of all our citizens. Furthermore, if we are ever to understand ourselves, our values, and our ways of defining reality, we must encounter those understandings, values, and definitions in the books we read.

Since the first edition of *Kaleidoscope,* our lives have been touched by recent immigrants who have survived war, death, and privation. These same folks, young and old, astonish us with their resilience and optimism as they learn to read, write, and think in a new language. Since the first edition of *Kaleidoscope,* all Americans have also faced national tragedies. These changes in the United States catalyzed a change in the format of this issue of *Kaleidoscope.* Our collaborative group of teachers, professors, and school administrators agreed that our edition would categorize the annotations and chapters by crucial issues rather than by genre. The following overview provides glimpses into the contents of each of the issue-oriented chapters.

Overview

For four hundred years, our society has been nourished and sustained by bilingual and multilingual families. This tradition continues today. We as a nation are indeed fortunate to have this linguistic richness. Tragically, for the same period our society has also been home to children who have witnessed lynchings, beatings, and violence visited on families simply because of the color of their skin or their religious practices. Today we harbor recent immigrant families who have lived these same horrors, but now we have the knowledge and skills to cultivate and nurture the confidence and resilience of their children.

Literature is one of our most powerful vehicles in this process. At its best, literature affirms life experiences. It offers models for coping with tragedy, and it also bridges differences in people's life experiences while turning our vision inward. In so doing, we can both examine and modify our own worldviews. We can keep growing.

Chapter 1, "Bilingual and Multilingual Literature," was organized by two Spanish-immersion teachers who are, happily, multilingual themselves. Because adults often have few accurate bibliographies for bilingual/multilingual literature, the chapter editors brought their expertise and experience to both selecting the books for the chapter and writing the annotations.

Chapter 2, "War and Resilience," presents accounts of young people as they face the many permutations of war. In these books, the characters model resilience—the ability to face tribulation yet maintain a balanced center of strength and perseverance. Our troubled times of violence on the playground and in schools need stories that are compelling illustrations of the strength and courage in each of us.

Chapter 3, "Social Responsibility," identifies books whose characters are caring, masterful, and realistic. The stories are peopled by youngsters and adults who not only empathize with others but also act on their empathy as they adopt or adapt to others' perspectives. Rather than taking a "Gee, I feel sorry for you, you poor thing" attitude, they advance the concept of setting aside the self and "becoming" the other person. As Meltzer writes, "If we don't have the capacity to think ourselves into another's skin, then we are in deep trouble in this polyglot nation" (Saul, 1994, p. 96).

Chapter 4, "Families, Friends, and Community," highlights books that convey us into the personal lives of the characters as they deal with others in social and personal relationships. These stories bridge all groups of diverse people for, regardless of how we define our roles within the family, group of friends, or community, we share the realities of struggling with these relationships.

Chapter 5, "Informative and Educational Books," treats nonfiction accounts as resources for learning and teaching. We cannot neglect these important resources for, as Joyce Hansen (2001) states, "primary sources are the heart and soul of any story." Only by drawing youngsters into the richness of nonfiction can we help students understand the backgrounds of fictional characters. Not only can good nonfiction be good reading, but it also helps readers construct an almost tangible context for the people they might encounter in fiction or poetry.

The final chapter, "Visibility," directs us to wonder how we would feel if we looked in the mirror and saw either no reflection or an unfamiliar image of someone who bore no resemblance to us. Imagine the confusion of children who never find people like themselves in the books they read. But simply adding color to book illustrations or accepting a book because it includes depictions of a non-European ethnic group is irresponsible. We must beware of books in which, for example, "Asian Americans are foreigners who all look alike and choose to live together in quaint communities in the midst of larger cities and cling to outworn alien customs" (Aoki, 1992, p. 113). Realistic literary images of ourselves, our lives, our families, our friends, and our communities affirm our existence—we can feel the warmth of our own breath and the rhythm of our heart on an astronomical scale. Our feelings of self-worth and self-esteem burgeon.

But it is equally important that we all are or can be enriched by the diversity of our many worlds and life roles. Anything less blinds us to the dizzying depth and blissful beauty of life. In our pursuit of diverse stories and reflections, however, we must be careful that those literary representations are appropriate and accurate. Therefore, we need criteria for selecting books.

Before we get to criteria selection, however, we wanted to lay out the organization of the annotations. As in previous editions, each annotation begins with the author, book title, publisher, year of publication, and ISBN—all the information helpful for finding these works in libraries and bookstores. Then we have included number of pages or identified the book as unpaged. To help teachers and librarians gauge whether a particular book is appropriate for a particular young reader, we have identified reading level. The basic genre—such as fiction, non-fiction, and biography—is identified next. Finally, when we have information about the author's ethnicity, we specify whether the book is an example of ethnic-specific, cross-cultural, or world literature. After the annotation itself, we have listed titles of other chapters in which the book could have been included. The initials of the contributor(s) who wrote the book summary round off the annotation, although when a book has won an award, the name of the award has been appended to the very end of the annotation.

Criteria Used in Selecting Books for Annotation

As in previous editions, most of the annotated books were sent to NCTE by their publishers, all of whom identified their publications as multicultural literature. Because less than 3 percent of the books published each year are written by or about people of color (Philip Lee, personal communication), the pool of books is small. For a three-year period, 1999–2001, the committee selected books for annotation from among those received from publishers. Many of the books, however, were purchased personally by our contributors who noticed both their presence in bookstores and their absence from our collection.

The committee's criteria for deciding which books we would and would not include for annotation have been widely used by librarians, families, and teachers (Hansen-Krening, 1992; Hansen-Krening & Mizokawa, 1997):

- *Is it a good story?* If the story isn't well written, it won't capture the reader's attention. If it doesn't capture the reader's attention, then it won't be enjoyed, puzzled over, remembered, or shared with others.

- *Do members of the specific ethnic group targeted in the story embrace the book?* Obviously, if the majority of folks from the book's focal ethnic group do not believe the book is accurate or effective, then it did not remain in this bibliography.

- *Is the author considered an authority not only on the ethnic group targeted in the story but also on the intricacies of diversity within that group?* If not, then once again the book's value should be questioned. Stereotyping blatantly ignores the uniqueness of individuals and instead portrays, states, or implies that everyone is alike. A story that presents, for example, all African Americans as urban dwellers, or all European Americans as rednecks, should be avoided.

- *Do the illustrations accurately portray the ethnic group?* The illustrations must be true to the time, the location, and the people portrayed. If, for example, all Native Americans are depicted wearing long braids, turquoise jewelry, and feathers in their hair, the book should be removed from our booklist.

- *Does the story have themes that bridge diverse perspectives?* Readers must feel connected to the stories they read, and generally it is the perceived theme of a book that provides that essential bridge between the life experiences of the reader(s) and the lives of the characters. Without the bridging theme, without that connection, the story is meaningless; we feel and learn nothing.

- *Does the book build self-esteem?* Any book that undermines, damages, distorts, or diminishes a reader's feelings of self-worth is unacceptable.

- *Does the writing help the reader examine his or her own attitudes and perspectives without imposing didactic views?* Great stories often help us to be introspective. Help is not what is offered if an external entity, by fiat and decree, imposes someone else's structure on our reality.

- *Is the book **ethnic-specific** literature, **cross-cultural** literature, or **world** literature?* Those of us working in this field soon discover the lack of correlation between what happens here in the United States and what happens in other countries. In U.S. history, assigning students to read stories set in Japan will not reflect the experiences of Japanese Americans. African myths do not portray the religious beliefs of African Americans. These are examples of *world literature:* about or reports on other countries. *Cross-cultural* stories are those written by an outsider looking into and attempting to write from the perspective of a specific ethnic group other than his or her own. Attempting to do so is tricky and often fails disastrously. *Ethnic-specific* literature is work written from an insider's perspective—that is, stories about an ethnic group told by a member of that ethnic group. Though not a guarantee that the story is good or even that members of that group embrace it, an ethnic-specific book might have a compelling authenticity to commend it. The committee has done its best to identify, in the bibliographical information, whether the book is ethnic-specific, cross-cultural, or world literature. As Bishop cautions,

> My claim here is not that an author from one group cannot write worthwhile books about another group, but that the resulting literature is likely not to be claimed by members of the featured group as *their* literature. Reading the literature of insiders will help teachers learn to recognize recurring themes, topics, values, attitudes and language features, social mores—-those elements that characterize the body of literature the group claims as its own. It will also acquaint them with the variety and diversity to be found *within* the culture. (1992, pp. 46–47)

And Now . . .

Lest there be any confusion, none of the books included in this edition of *Kaleidoscope* is recommended as an add-on to a corpus of literature; they are intended for inclusion as part of the whole, the canon of literature students are expected to read. They bring *unity through diversity* (Hansen-Krening & Mizokawa, 1993), an approach that has come to characterize general curricula. Ethnic-specific, cross-cultural, and world literature should be an inseparable part of the curriculum at every grade level.

Although this is the last edition of *Kaleidoscope,* the move toward a more inclusive canon must continue, even without this historically valuable resource. Literature—a truly *American* literature—can open the hearts and minds of all. Against the temptation to consider literature "only words," not sticks and stones that can hurt you, Joyce Hansen (2001) says, "Broken bones heal; broken spirits are passed from generation to generation."

References

Aoki, E. (1992). Turning the page: Asian Pacific American children's literature. In V. J. Harris (Ed.), *Teaching multicultural literature in grades K–8* (p. 13). Norwood, MA: Christopher-Gordon.

Bishop, R. S. (1982). *Shadow and substance: Afro-American experience in contemporary children's fiction.* Urbana, IL: National Council of Teachers of English.

Bishop, R. S. (1992). Multicultural literature for children: Making informed choices. In V. J. Harris (Ed.), *Teaching multicultural literature in grades K–8* (pp. 46–47). Norwood, MA: Christopher-Gordon.

Bishop, R. S. (1994). *Kaleidoscope: A multicultural booklist for grades K–8.* Urbana, IL: National Council of Teachers of English.

Hansen, J. (2001, May 1). *Imagining the past: Writing historical fiction and non-fiction for young people.* Paper presented at the 46th Annual Convention of the International Reading Association, New Orleans, LA.

Hansen-Krening, N. (1992). Authors of color: A multicultural perspective. *Journal of Reading, 36*(2), 124–29.

Hansen-Krening, N., & Mizokawa, D. T. (1993). *From diversity to unity: A national American literature.* Seattle: University of Washington. Grant proposal to the Fund for the Improvement of Post-Secondary Education.

Hansen-Krening, N., & Mizokawa, D. T. (1997). Exploring ethnic-specific literature: A unity of parents, families, and educators. *Journal of Adolescent & Adult Literacy, 41,* 180–89.

Mizokawa, D. T. (1992, April). The problem with lumping data. In J. Ogbu (Critic) & C. Walker (Moderator), *Why Asian American students succeed academically (or do they?).* Symposium conducted at the annual meeting of the American Educational Research Association, San Francisco.

Mizokawa, D. T., & Ryckman, D. B. (1990). Attributions of academic success and failure: A comparison of six Asian-American ethnic groups. *Journal of Cross-Cultural Psychology, 21,* 434–51.

Saul, E. W. (Ed.) (1994). *Nonfiction for the classroom: Milton Meltzer on writing, history, and social responsibility.* New York: Teachers College Press.

1 Bilingual and Multilingual Literature

Deborah Hinton and R. Debbie Bier

Over one hundred years ago, the United States was in the midst of an industrial revolution, during which new technology, industries, and products helped bring about a new way of life. These changes, though not always welcome, resulted in better living conditions for most people. Now, over a century later, we are on the brink of a cultural revolution, a revolution in which diversity and appreciation of both similarities and differences are key to an inclusive, tolerant society. Our society is finally realizing that not every person is the same and not every person has the same background; more important, more and more people now acknowledge that the unique qualities of each culture should be celebrated and sustained.

Bilingual and multilingual literature emphasizes different cultures, teaching children that languages other than their native ones are not to be feared or ridiculed but rather to be respected and admired. Instead of viewing other languages as gibberish that can be written off as "weird" or "funny," bilingual literature teaches children that other languages are as complex and sophisticated as their own language. As we move into this cultural revolution, bilingual and multilingual literature is integral to bringing about understanding and acceptance of the diversity all around us. No one language is either more or less complex than any other, and this message must be brought to all children. In *The Rainbow Tulip* (1999), about a Mexican American child who struggles with the difficulties of participating in two cultures, Pat Mora summarizes this dilemma in the simple sentence, "It is hard to be different. It is sweet and sour, like lime sherbet." But if society is truly ready to embrace the principle that differences do not have to be negative, then bilingual and multilingual literature is key to the understanding and acceptance of all cultures within U.S. society. The cultural diversity of the United States grows and expands every day, and education and literature must grow along with it.

The following annotations are of stories translated into one or more languages within the same bound pages, or of books that have another lingual counterpart. Also included in this category are books written primarily in one language but that incorporate other languages. Our hope is that the literature in this chapter will promote appreciation of the uniqueness of different peoples, cultures, and their languages.

Reference

Mora, P. (1999). *The rainbow tulip.* New York: Viking.

1.1   Alarcón, Francisco X. **Angels Ride Bikes and Other Fall Poems/ Los ángeles andan en bicicleta y otros poemas de otoño.** Illustrated by Maya Christina Gonzalez. Children's Book Press, 1999. ISBN 0-89239-160-X. 32 pp. Primary–Intermediate. Fiction, Ethnic specific.

"These poems celebrate Los Angeles as a Promised Land where people from all over the world make their dreams come true," says the author. This bilingual collection of poems by renowned Mexican American poet Francisco Alarcón revisits and celebrates his childhood memories of growing up in Los Angeles, focusing on the simple joys and trials of everyday life. The characters portrayed by illustrator Gonzalez are actual photographs of friends, relatives, and strangers that she copied and painted over. Gonzalez's exquisite artwork complements each poem, bringing to life the people and places of Alarcón's childhood. The author dedicates this book to his mother, "who taught us the real meaning of '¡Sí se puede!' (Yes, you can do it!)." (Families, Friends, and Community) DH & DB

1.2   Alarcón, Francisco X. **Iguanas in the Snow and Other Winter Poems/Iguanas en la nieve y otros poemas de invierno.** Illustrated by Maya Christina Gonzalez. Children's Book Press, 2001. ISBN 0-89239-168-5. 32 pp. Primary–Intermediate. Fiction, Ethnic specific.

These poems describe northern California, where author Francisco Alarcón has lived for more than two decades. His bilingual collection of poems celebrates winter in San Francisco as well as the mountains of northern California. Through beautifully illustrated collages, Gonzalez creates a lively background to complement the author's magical words. (Families, Friends, and Community) DH & DB

1.3   Elya, Susan Middleton. **Say Hola to Spanish at the Circus.** Illustrated by Loretta Lopez. Lee & Low, 2000. ISBN 1-880000-92-X. Unpaged. Primary. Nonfiction, Cross-cultural.

Come to the circus and "bring tu mamá, and tus hermanos, abuelos, papá" to learn Spanish in a fun and inventive way! Susan Elya returns for a third time in her Say Hola to Spanish series, bringing to life the Spanish language in an innovative fashion by integrating Spanish rhyming words on every page. This is an excellent resource for learning new vocabulary in the primary grades. (Informative and Educational Books) DH & DB

1.4   Emberley, Rebecca. **My Colors/Mis colores.** Illustrated by Rebecca Emberley. Little, Brown, 2000. ISBN 0-316-23347-1. Unpaged. Primary. Nonfiction.

This primary board book provides a collection of colors using both Spanish and English words. The illustrations are simple yet appealing for very young beginning learners. This is one in a series of four books by Emberley. Others include *My Shapes/Mis formas, My Numbers/Mis números,* and *My Opposites/Mis opuestos.* (Informative and Educational Books) DH & DB

1.5   Emberley, Rebecca. **My Numbers/Mis numeros.** Illustrated by Rebecca Emberley. Little, Brown, 2000. ISBN 0-316-23350-1. Unpaged. Primary. Nonfiction.

This primary board book provides numbers from one to ten in both Spanish and English using the proper nouns that designate the numbers. The illustrations are simple yet appealing for very young beginning learners. (Informative and Educational Books) DH & DB

1.6   Emberley, Rebecca. **My Opposites/Mis opuestos.** Illustrated by Rebecca Emberley. Little, Brown, 2000. ISBN 0-316-23345-5. Unpaged. Primary. Nonfiction.

This useful primary board book focuses on words in both Spanish and English that describe opposites. The illustrations are simple yet appealing for very young beginning learners. (Informative and Educational Books) DH & DB

1.7   Emberley, Rebecca. **My Shapes/Mis formas.** Illustrated by Rebecca Emberley. Little, Brown, 2000. ISBN 0-316-23355-2. Unpaged. Primary. Nonfiction.

This primary board book offers a collection of shapes in both Spanish and English. The illustrations are simple yet appealing for very young beginning learners. (Informative & Educational) DH & DB

1.8   Fine, Edith Hope. **Under the Lemon Moon.** Illustrated by René King Moreno. Lee & Low, 1999. ISBN 1-88-0000-69-5. Unpaged. Primary. Fiction.

"Who is the Night Man? Why does he take my lemons?" Rosalinda, with her pet hen, Blanca, sets out to seek the one person who can answer her questions and help save her sick tree. Rosalinda finds *La Anciana,* the Old One, who offers Rosalinda the solution to her predicament. This touching story about generosity and forgiveness includes a Spanish-English glossary. This book is also published in a separate Spanish edition. (Families, Friends, and Community) DH & DB

1.9   Freschet, Gina. **Naty's Parade.** Illustrated by Gina Freschet. Farrar, Straus, and Giroux, 2000. ISBN 0-374-35500-2. Unpaged. Primary. Fiction, World.

Guelaguetza, a cultural festival of folkloric dances, is celebrated on the last two Mondays of July in Oaxaca, Mexico. Naty, dressed in her mouse costume, is excited to be dancing in the fiesta parade—until "*¡Ay, caramba!* She's lost!" and she cannot find the parade. Bold-color drawings complement this enchanting story. A Spanish edition, *La procesión de Naty,* is also available. (Families, Friends, and Community) DH & DB

1.10   Garza, Carmen Lomas. **Magic Windows/Ventanas mágicas.** Illustrated by Carmen Lomas Garza. Children's Book Press, 1999. ISBN 0-89239-157-X. 32 pp. Intermediate. Nonfiction, Ethnic specific.

"These pictures are like magic windows. When you look through them, you can see into another world." This book by award-winning artist Carmen Lomas Garza is a bilingual portrayal of her experiences and life as an artist, as well as an integration of Aztec legends. Garza takes the reader on a fascinating exploration of her family, community, and ancestors through the traditional folk art form of *papel picado* (cut-paper art). (Informative and Educational Books) DH & DB

1.11 Krahn, Fernando. **La familia Numerozzi.** Illustrated by Fernando Krahn. Ediciones Ekaré, 2000. ISBN 980-257-247-0. Unpaged. Primary. Fiction, Ethnic specific.

The Numerozzi family is full of surprises in this humorous, original story written in Spanish. This family of fictional animals will delight early primary students through their comical adventures and inventions. (Families, Friends, and Community) DH & DB

1.12 Miller, William. **Zora Hurston y el árbol soñador.** Illustrated by Cornelius Van Wright and Ying-Hwa Hu. Lee & Low, 2001. ISBN 1-58430-030-2. Unpaged. Primary–Intermediate. Nonfiction, Cross-cultural.

This biography of the renowned African American writer Zora Neale Hurston is an excellent Spanish translation of the book *Zora Hurston and the Chinaberry Tree.* The story focuses on a specific period in Hurston's life and explores her relationship with her mother, who inspired her daughter to develop her free spirit and who affirmed the unlimited possibilities of life. This book is exquisitely illustrated with beautiful watercolors. (Informative and Educational Books) DH & DB

1.13 Nikola-Lisa, W. **America: A Book of Opposites/America: Un libro de contrarios.** Illustrated by Hector Viveros Lee, Yvonne Buchanan, Adjoa J. Burrowes, Enrique O. Sanchez, Darryl Ligasan, Keunhee Lee, Anna Rich, Michelle Reiko Kumata, Erwin Printup Jr., and Gregory Christie. Lee & Low, 2001. ISBN 1-58430-028-0. Unpaged. Primary. Nonfiction, Ethnic specific.

This sweet bilingual board book is a delight to hold and read, and offers gorgeous illustrations on every page. The various faces of the people, landscapes, living creatures, activities, and transportation that can be found in the United States are the highlight of this educational book. It's a durable and informative book for the teacher of young readers. (Families, Friends, and Community) DH & DB

1.14 Pérez, Amada Irma. **My Very Own Room/Mi propio cuartito.** Illustrated by Maya Christina Gonzalez. Children's Book Press, 2000. ISBN 0-89239-164 -2. 32 pp. Primary–Intermediate. Fiction.

"Aha. This is it! This could be my room." This is the touching story of a young Mexican American girl who more than anything in the world wants a room of her own. In this bilingual book based on her own family story, Amada Pérez teaches us about the strength of a family and the importance of dreams. Through colorful, bold paintings, illustrator Gonzalez brings the scenes to life. (Families, Friends, and Community) DH & DB

1.15   Pilkey, Dav. **Dragón y el gato panzón.** Illustrated by Dav Pilkey. Ediciones Ekaré, 1999. ISBN 980-257-218-7. 48 pp. Primary. Fiction.

This charming and lighthearted tale is an excellent Spanish translation of the book *Dragon's Fat Cat*, the heartwarming story of the relationship between a dragon and a cat. This chapter book will keep young readers captivated and provides an excellent segue into the topic of friendship. The illustrations are simple and endearing. (Families, Friends, and Community) DH & DB

1.16   Rodríguez, Luis J. **It Doesn't Have to Be This Way: A Barrio Story/No tiene que ser así: Una historia del barrio.** Illustrated by Daniel Galvez. Children's Book Press, 1999. ISBN 0-89239-161-8. 31 pp. Intermediate. Fiction, Ethnic specific.

"It doesn't have to be this way, *m'ijo*," said Tío Rogelio. "I know you want to be a man, but you have to decide what kind of a man you want to be." When Monchi is told by a member of a local barrio gang that it is time to join up, he is excited yet reluctant. He must "prove himself" in order to be accepted. After Monchi becomes more involved in the gang's activities, a tragic event forces him to make an important decision about the course of his life. Presented in both English and Spanish, this compelling and inspiring story, which author Luis Rodríguez knows firsthand, makes a lasting impression on the reader. (Families, Friends, and Community) DH & DB

1.17   Schecter, Ellen. **The Family Haggadah.** Illustrated by Neil Waldman. Viking, 1999. ISBN 0-670-88341-7. 66 pp. Primary–Intermediate. Nonfiction, Ethnic specific.

This book provides an excellent explanation of the celebration of Passover from the night before the Seder until after the meal. It includes specific suggestions about ways to help children participate in the ceremony. In *The Family Haggadah*, Schecter deliberately avoids sexist language, usage, and customs. Traditional texts appear in English, Hebrew, and Hebrew transliteration. (Informative and Educational Books) DH & DB

1.18 Vargo, Sharon Hawkins. **Señor Felipe's Alphabet Adventure/El alfabeto Español.** Illustrated by Sharon Hawkins Vargo. Milbrook, 2000. ISBN 0-7613-1860-7. Unpaged. Primary. Fiction.

Señor Felipe is given the mission of photographing things that begin with each letter of the Spanish alphabet, and off he goes to complete his assignment. This Spanish-English bilingual alphabet book takes the reader from *A* to *Z* through comical adventures for photographer Señor Felipe and his trusty parrot Paco. A Spanish-English glossary and phonetic pronunciation guide are included. (Informative and Educational Books) DH & DB

2 War and Resilience

Carolyn W. Jackson and Kipchoge Kirkland

In times of war, many of us, young and old, wrestle with the tensions of and threats to justice, freedom, and humanity. We may draw on our deepest held philosophical values and spiritual/moral foundations to help us make sense of the tragedies that begin and end in battle. Developing an understanding of war may also help readers develop a keen sense of democracy, political reality, and perhaps a critical understanding of what it takes to encourage or destroy human dignity. *Fighting for Honor: Japanese Americans and World War II* (Cooper, 2000), for instance, demonstrates that while facing the ironies and contradictions of social discrimination and a governmental policy that betrayed them, many Japanese Americans remained valiant. In essence, confronting war however it is presented is no easy task. The depth of the human spirit, however, continues to reveal itself in the many ways in which diverse cultural groups have been resilient in times of conflict, tragedy, and loss. Reading literature about these experiences can certainly help us learn from the past in order to positively influence the future.

Choosing literature about war and resilience for children and young adults is a daunting responsibility. Authors treat war in different literal and metaphoric ways, which makes selecting such material a challenge to find texts that are engaging, honest, fair, thought-provoking, and, more important, developmentally appropriate. Nancy Day's *Your Travel Guide to Civil War America* (2001), for example, which presents an important, literal, and graphic journey through the historic conflict between North and South, is written so that any middle school student can successfully embark on the historical trek to gain deeper insight into the impact of civil war on the United States. A book that incorporates both metaphoric and literal tensions of war is *The War Within: A Novel of the Civil War* (Matas, 2001). Hannah is a Jewish girl who wrestles with the consequences of her belief that African Americans are inferior. She struggles to make sense of the war and abolitionists while the Jews in her community are targeted and discriminated against by the government. This Civil War novel demonstrates the blurred line between the enemy we imagine and the actual enemy, when we are forced to examine our own perspectives, roles, actions, and contributions to society.

The daughters of an Ojibway family in *The Birchbark House* (Erdrich, 1999) experience a metaphorical war when they grapple with a smallpox epidemic and find their true identities, inner strength, and destinies. In these kinds of war stories, characters' resilience is evident in what they endure, what they embrace, what they leave behind, and what they find. In other instances, war and resilience are demonstrated in the poetic rhythms of children's songs, such as those shared in Alice McGill's *In the Hollow of Your Hand: Slave Lullabies* (2000). In this euphonic book, McGill's generational family songs reflect an emerging resilience of strength, courage, and laughter, and a bold pride that has endured battles of slavery, discrimination, and both physical and psychological warfare.

The purpose of choosing war and resilience literature for children and young adults is to help them confront different perspectives in a manner that does not prevent them from asking the question "Why?" No child should be prohibited from challenging our practices of justice, equality, and democracy when they see for themselves that these ideals are not being realized. Children are our most important investment in the future. Their sense of fairness in our darkest moments of struggle may mean the difference between building a collective community and living forever divided in isolation. It is our hope that the material presented in this chapter of *Kaleidoscope* will challenge readers to maintain their commitment to justice and freedom while simultaneously recognizing that being resilient is one of our childhood attributes that may help us deal with both the interior and exterior realities of war.

2.1   Alshalabi, Firyal. **Summer of 1990.** Aunt Strawberry, 1999. ISBN 0-9669988-0-4. 138 pp. Intermediate. Fiction, World.

Danah realizes her dream to leave Kuwait for a short summer visit to a beloved uncle. Her joyful time in New York is cut short by the terror of Iraq's invasion of Kuwait and the uncertain status of her family. Danah begins her quest to find and be reunited with her mother, father, brother, and sister. From the perspective of a teenager, the Gulf War has an immediacy that takes readers into the tragic realities faced by too many of our world's adolescents. (Social Responsibility; Families, Friends, and Community) NHK

2.2   Asgedom, Mawi. **Of Beetles and Angels: A True Story of the American Dream.** Megadee, 2001. ISBN 0-9704982-6-8. 148 pp. Middle school. Nonfiction, Ethnic specific.

Surviving genocide in one's own country is remarkable enough, but in this story a young man tells about how his family escaped certain death by making the incredible trek from Ethiopia to a refugee camp in the Sudan. After years in the camp, the family immigrated to the United States. Life was only somewhat safer once his family reached the United States, yet the author never loses faith in the future. The success he achieves through determination, hope, resilience, and family love culminates in his graduation from Harvard. This is an inspiring story for all readers. (Social Responsibility; Families, Friends, and Community; Visibility) NHK

2.3   Burrowes, Adjoa J. **Grandma's Purple Flowers.** Illustrated by Adjoa J. Burrowes. Lee & Low, 2000. ISBN 1-880000-73-3. Unpaged. Primary. Fiction, Ethnic specific.

A little girl visits her beloved grandmother and celebrates the beauty of nature with her. With seasonal changes, the grandmother falters. When she dies, the little girl grieves but eventually celebrates grandmother's memory with spring's first purple flowers. The gentle story opens up opportunities for adults to talk about death and dying with curious or worried children. (Families, Friends, and Community) NHK

2.4   Chen, Da. **China's Son: Growing Up in the Cultural Revolution.** Delacorte, 2001. ISBN 0-385-72929-4. 213 pp. Upper elementary. Autobiography, World.

As difficult as it may have been to achieve, Chen has written a breezy account of his young life during and after the Cultural Revolution in China. As he notes, this is just one of many first-person accounts of that period in China's history. For a balanced picture of that time, some of those other accounts should be included, because Chen's narrative doesn't touch on the extreme danger and suffering that many Chinese experienced during the Cultural Revolution. NHK

2.5   Coleman, Evelyn. **Born in Sin.** Atheneum, 2001. ISBN 0-689-83833-6. 234 pp. Middle school. Fiction, Ethnic specific.

Resilient describes Keisha, her family, and many of her friends. Coleman unfailingly entrances readers of any age by the authenticity of her characters and the lives they lead. She neither demonizes nor lionizes any one ethnic group while carefully laying bare the conflicts that many African American youngsters encounter on a daily basis. Keisha fights for her right to an education and for her future even after she is labeled an "at risk" student. She is not alone in this fight, for she is loved and cared for. This is a superior book for a read-aloud and discussion. (Families, Friends, and Community) NHK

2.6   Coleman, Evelyn. **Circle of Fire.** Pleasant Company, 2001. ISBN 1-58485-339-5. 150 pp. Ages 8–13. Fiction, Ethnic specific.

The author notes in the afterword "Looking Back: 1958" that she drew from a true story in creating the lives of African American and European American families during the violence visited on African American families by the Ku Klux Klan. Mendy, the protagonist, has a strong and happy friendship with a White boy, which sets the conflict of the story. Add to this mix the Klan's plan to raid a meeting at which former First Lady Eleanor Roosevelt is to speak, and you have a story sure to captivate. This would be an excellent book for literature circles in classrooms studying U.S. history. (Social Responsibility; Families, Friends, and Community) NHK

2.7   Collier, Christopher, and James Lincoln Collier. **Slavery and the Coming of the Civil War, 1831–1861.** Benchmark, 2000. ISBN 0-7614-0817-7. 81 pp. Intermediate–Middle school. Nonfiction.

The Colliers discuss pivotal events and pervasive sentiments leading up to the Civil War, as well as key players who planted the seeds for war and articulated the justification for the institution of slavery. The authors have included various examples of contemporary anti–African American sentiment, such as cartoons and posters that demanded the return of free African Americans to slavery. This text also includes information about slave trade routes, a bibliography, and an index. (Social Responsibility; Informative and Educational Books) CWJ

2.8   Cooper, Michael L. **Fighting for Honor: Japanese Americans and World War II.** Clarion, 2000. ISBN 0-395-91375-6. 104 pp. Middle school. Nonfiction, Cross-cultural.

Cooper taps a variety of resources such as personal diaries and national, state, military, and Library of Congress archives to examine the unfair treatment and relocation of Japanese Americans to internment camps during World War II. He also features the frequently overlooked role of Japanese Americans who valiantly served in the U.S. military despite American propaganda that dehumanized and justified poor treatment of Japanese Americans. This book contains a chronology of events, endnotes, bibliographical references, and an index. (Social Responsibility; Informative and Educational Books) CWJ

2.9 Cox, Clinton. **Come All You Brave Soldiers: Blacks in the Revolutionary War.** Scholastic, 1999. ISBN 0-590-47576-2. 182 pp. Middle school. Nonfiction.

Using primary and secondary sources, Cox celebrates the contributions of unsung African American Revolutionary War soldiers such as Lemuel Haynes, Peter Salem, and Sampson Talbert. These men and thousands of other overlooked Black veterans viewed serving in the army as a chance to gain U.S. citizenship and thus equality. Cox shows how these beliefs and efforts were eventually betrayed when many African American soldiers were enslaved or reenslaved after they fought for their country and their freedom. This text also contains illustrations, bibliographic references, and an index. (Visibility; Informative and Educational Books) CWJ

2.10 Curtis, Christopher Paul. **Bud, Not Buddy.** Delacorte, 1999. 245 pp. ISBN 0-385-32306-9. Intermediate–Middle school. Fiction, Ethnic specific.

As in his first book, *The Watsons Go to Birmingham,* Curtis makes history come alive. During the Depression, ten-year-old Bud sets out on a quest to find his father, a well-known African American musician. During his search, this resilient boy finds himself. Boys and girls alike will be absorbed in Bud's story. (Friends, Families, and Community) NHK

Newbery Medal and Coretta Scott King Award, 2000; International Reading Association Children's Book Award, 2000

2.11 Day, Nancy. **Your Travel Guide to Civil War America.** Runestone, 2001. ISBN 0-8225-3078-3. 96 pp. Middle school. Nonfiction.

Day takes the reader on a journey back into Civil War times. Based on many firsthand reports and the research of historians, archaeologists, and other experts, this informative text reveals key players, covert operations, and numerous aspects of the social and political climate during this historic period. Readers may be surprised to learn that many women secretly enlisted in the Union and Confederate armies disguised as men. This text also includes activities, bibliographic references, a glossary, and an index. (Informative and Educational Books) MVW

2.12   Diouf, Sylviane A. **Growing Up in Slavery.** Millbrook, 2001. ISBN 0-7613-1763-5. 96 pp. Intermediate–Adult. Nonfiction.

This thorough examination of life for child slaves in the United States gives readers a complete overview of the conditions children endured before and during captivity. It is an accurate and vivid portrayal of the abuse, violence, injustice, racism, and separation from family that forced them to learn how to become resilient, physically and mentally strong, and ultimately great contributors to U.S. society. According to the author, "Their abundant creativity gave America gifted poets, writers, inventors, musicians, painters, scholars, and orators. The children who grew up in slavery were hardy survivors and unsung heroes." MVW

2.13   Equiano, Olaudah. Adapted by Ann Cameron. **The Kidnapped Prince: The Life of Olaudah Equiano.** Knopf, 2000. ISBN 0-375-80346-7. 145 pp. Intermediate–Adult. Nonfiction.

This adapted version of one of the first North American slave narratives, by Olaudah Equiano, tells the chilling story of how a young boy struggled through his experiences as a child slave through several owners. He eloquently expresses a life of betrayal and abuse, depression and exhaustion—physical, emotional, and mental—in the fight to gain his freedom. A map and other illustrations of Equiano's experiences are included and will confirm for readers the reality of his life. The original story, titled *The Interesting Narrative of the Life of Olaudah Equiano*, has been read by people around the world and was a bestseller in the late 1700s. MVW

2.14   Erdrich, Louise. **The Birchbark House.** Hyperion, 1999. ISBN 0-7868-0300-2. 239 pp. Intermediate–Middle school. Historical fiction, Ethnic specific.

In this historical novel, the daughters of an Ojibway family find their true identities through the privation and hardship brought on by a smallpox epidemic. The eldest daughter learns that she needn't depend on her beauty as her only strength as she brings literacy to her family. The younger daughter finds her destiny as a healer. After overcoming the horrors of the epidemic, the villagers rebuild their lives just as they rebuild their birchbark homes. (Social Responsibility; Visibility) NHK

Jane Addams Honor Book, 2000

2.15 Fradin, Dennis Brindell, and Judith Bloom Fradin. **Ida B. Wells: Mother of the Civil Rights Movement.** Clarion, 2000. ISBN 0-395-89898-6. 168 pp. Middle school. Nonfiction, Biography.

"The words GOD BLESS HER is written here on every acre of ground, and on every doorstep, and inside of every home." Readers will fervently echo the sentiment behind this sharecropper's tribute to Ida B. Wells, a major figure of the early civil rights movement, best remembered today as a tireless social activist who helped put an end to lynching. This excellent biography is enriched with passages from Wells's diaries, letters, and newspaper articles. Wells never hesitated to confront any person—from local sheriffs to Booker T. Washington to Woodrow Wilson—who she felt had failed to act for justice. (Social Responsibility; Informative & Educational) NHK

2.16 Gottfried, Ted. **Children of the Slaughter: Young People of the Holocaust.** Illustrated by Stephen Alcorn. Twenty-First Century, 2001. ISBN 0-761-31716-3. 112 pp. Middle–High school. Nonfiction.

This nonfiction account of the Holocaust is filled with heartbreaking information on and pictures of child victims, not only Jewish but also German children. Teachers can help students think about what we can learn from the Holocaust and what we can do to prevent anything like it from happening again. The book invites discussion of the consequences of prejudice and what young people can do to combat it in themselves as well as in society. (Social Responsibility; Visibility) IL

2.17 Greene, Meg. **Slave Young, Slave Long: The American Slave Experience.** Lerner, 1999. ISBN 0-8225-1739-6. 88 pp. Intermediate. Nonfiction.

This factual documentation of slavery in the United States details the historical development of Jim Crow laws and practices that African Americans endured for over two hundred years. Primary sources such as personal letters and accounts, famous quotes, original pictures, and slave songs illuminate the daily realities of their struggles for freedom and continued hope for a just society. Also included are advertisements for slave auctions, information about African American Union soldiers and life in slave quarters, and post–Civil War family photos. This book exposes the intimate lives of African Americans throughout the years of Jim Crow and honors the level of strength it took to tolerate overt and insidious discrimination. MVW

2.18   Hansen, Joyce. **One True Friend.** Clarion, 2001. ISBN 0-395-84983-7. 154 pp. Upper elementary–Middle school. Fiction, Ethnic specific.

Joyce Hansen and her books are national treasures. Whether fiction or nonfiction, contemporary or stories of the past, Hansen's books draw readers into the hearts, souls, and minds of her characters. In *One True Friend*, she reunites us with Doris and Amir of her earlier *The Gift Giver* and *Yellow Bird and Me*. In this latest story, Doris copes with issues of peer pressure and self-identity. Amir struggles with the complex issues of coping with his little brother's complete absorption into foster care; going to live with the Smiths while also searching for his other brothers and sisters; unearthing true memories of life before his parents' deaths; and, finally, making a choice between foster families. Hansen enters her characters so honestly and completely that readers feel like they're living with them. She has also turned a story that could be sappy and overly sentimental into a tale of resilience in the face of life's obstacles. (Social Responsibility; Families, Friends, and Community) NHK

2.19   Hicyilmaz, Gaye. **Smiling for Strangers.** Farrar, Straus and Giroux, 2000. ISBN 0-374-37081-8. 152 pp. Middle school–High school. Fiction, World.

"[War] is about old men . . . sending young men . . . out to kill and be killed" (p. 141). Yet the impact of war devastates the lives of everyone involved. A case in point, fourteen-year-old Nina launches her long, lonely, dangerous, and desperate journey to find a secure place—England—from her war-torn motherland, Yugoslavia. As Nina searches for her mother's friend, Paul, who turns out to be Nina's brother's father, the story offers little snippets about helping others and being helped, hatred toward foreigners, and ignorance of foreign lands, all issues worth mulling over. (Social Responsibility; Families, Friends, and Community) IL

2.20 Holliday, Laurel, compiler. **Dreaming in Color, Living in Black and White: Our Own Stories of Growing Up Black in America.** Pocket, 2000. ISBN 0-671-04127-4. 199 pp. Middle school. Nonfiction, Ethnic specific.

Each of these stories is an individual's memory of encountering racism as a child or young adult. Both harrowing and truthful, these accounts are personal views of U.S. social history. The African American contributors represent a broad spectrum of socioeconomic and geographical backgrounds, but each shares the trauma and violence of racism, whether they are accused of being "too Black" or of being "too White." (Social Responsibility) NHK

2.21 Littlesugar, Amy. **Tree of Hope.** Illustrated by Floyd Cooper. Philomel, 1999. ISBN 0-399-23300-8. Unpaged. Primary–Intermediate. Historical fiction, Ethnic specific.

In this beautifully written and illustrated work of historical fiction, Florrie's father is an out-of-work Harlem actor who finally gets a part in Orson Welles's production of Macbeth—cast entirely with African American actors. Littlesugar irresistibly draws readers into this historical fiction through Florrie's love, pride, and hope in and for her father. (Visibility) NHK

2.22 Mah, Adeline Yen. **Chinese Cinderella: The True Story of an Unwanted Daughter.** Delacorte, 1999. ISBN 0-385-32707-2. 205 pp. Intermediate–Middle school. Nonfiction, World.

This children's version of the adult book *Falling Leaves* is no less harrowing in its honest depiction of life in China before and during the ascendance of the Chinese Communist Party and the Cultural Revolution. It is a story that models strength and courage for all children who feel unwanted and unaccepted. (Families, Friends, and Community) NHK

2.23   Marx, Trish. **One Boy from Kosovo.** Photographs by Cindy Karp. HarperCollins, 2000. ISBN 0-688-17733-6. 24 pp. Intermediate–Middle school. Nonfiction, World.

This photo-essay begins before Edi and his family were forced to leave their home in Kosovo: "The things he could do seemed wonderful to Edi. He went to school every day with his cousin and best friend, Shkurta, . . . he played sports, . . . he celebrated his twelfth birthday with his friends." But war changes Edi's life, engaging the reader's empathy with Edi's fear and loss. The photographs show that courage keeps hope alive even under unimaginable circumstances. *One Boy from Kosovo* is a simple and honorably told story. (Visibility; Families, Friends, and Community) NHK

2.24   Matas, Carol. **The War Within: A Novel of the Civil War.** Simon & Schuster, 2001. ISBN 0-689-82935-3. 151 pp. Intermediate–Middle school. Fiction.

The historical setting for this work of fiction is based on the official General Order that accused Jews of violating trade regulations during the Civil War. Hannah and her family are forced to leave their home in the South because they are Jews. Hannah has very strong views about the necessity of slavery and the inferiority of African Americans, but her beliefs are challenged when her sister begins to fall in love with a Union soldier and abolitionist. The clash between the sisters helps Hannah question her fundamental beliefs about the war, slavery, and humanity. (Social Responsibility; Informative and Educational Books) CWJ

2.25   McGill, Alice. **In the Hollow of Your Hand: Slave Lullabies.** Illustrated by Michael Cummings. Houghton Mifflin, 2000. ISBN 0-395-85755-4. 35 pp. All ages. Nonfiction.

McGill transcribes and sings songs collected from generations of family oral histories. These songs tell real-life stories and convey hope during times of despair, survival when death is near, and comfort in the belief that better times will come—"if not on earth, then in heaven." This text also contains sheet music and a CD of the lullabies sung by Alice McGill. (Informative and Educational Books; Families, Friends, and Community) CWJ

2.26   Meltzer, Milton. **They Came in Chains: The Story of the Slave Ships.** Benchmark, 2000. ISBN 0-7614-0967-X. 90 pp. Intermediate–Middle school. Nonfiction, Cross-cultural.

Meltzer describes the rise and decline of the African slave trade through a strong narrative and the use of numerous archival paintings, drawings, sale advertisements, maps, and other documents that reveal how slaves were captured, stowed, treated, and sold as property. He explains how slave traders justified their actions and profited from the mistreatment and sale of kidnapped Africans of all ages. Meltzer also describes the survival rates for slaves and the effects the slave trade had on West Africa, the Americas, and most of Europe. A bibliography and index are included. (Informative and Educational Books; Social Responsibility) CWJ

2.27   Miller, William. **The Piano.** Illustrated by Susan Keeter. Lee & Low, 2000. ISBN 1-880000989. Unpaged. Primary. Fiction, Cross-cultural.

Teachers will need to introduce this book carefully because it lends itself to radically different readings. On one level, this can be read as the stereotypical story of the gracious White benefactor who helps a poor little underprivileged girl who wants to hear "different music." On another level, the story is about friendship, mutual support, self-sacrifice, and generosity. A wealthy, elderly, southern White woman employs an African American child as a servant. The little girl wants to learn to play the piano and the elderly woman wants to teach her, but the woman's hands are crippled with pain, so the child massages them. When the child's co-worker, an African American boy, deserts his responsibilities, the little girl willingly assumes his heavy chores. The little girl's hands become stiff and sore, and the woman massages them. NHK

2.28   Noguchi, Rick, and Deneen Jenks. **Flowers from Mariko.** Illustrated by Michelle Reiko Kumata. Lee & Low, 2001. ISBN 1-58430-032-9. Unpaged. All ages. Fiction, Ethnic specific.

Mariko is one of the over 120,000 persons of Japanese heritage forced to live in an internment camp after the bombing of Pearl Harbor. Three years after having been interned, she and her family pack to leave the barbed-wire confines. They are free at last to make the transition back to their former lives. But after first settling into a temporary trailer park established for returning internees, their new lives still remind Mariko of camp. While Mariko's father slowly rebuilds his gardening business using discarded equipment, Mariko plants a flower garden that will give the family the courage and hope to persevere. With the teacher and other texts to provide a historical backdrop, this book can introduce younger students to the Japanese American experience in the United States during and after World War II. (Informative and Educational Books) EMA

2.29   Radin, Ruth Yaffe. **Escape to the Forest: Based on a True Story of the Holocaust.** Illustrated by Janet Hamlin. HarperCollins, 2000. ISBN 0-060-28520-6. 90 pp. Intermediate–High school. Fiction, World.

Based on the true story of a ten-year-old Jewish girl named Sarah who survived the German occupation of Lida, Poland, during the beginning of World War II, this fictional account of family ties, discrimination, fear, danger, pain, and hope unfolds as family members and neighbors take great risks to help one another survive. Realizing they will not survive by staying together, Sarah's parents support her escape to the forest, where Tuvia Bielski is secretly leading a mission to save Jewish lives. (Social Responsibility; Informative and Educational Books) CWJ

2.30   Schmidt, Gary. **Mara's Stories: Glimmers in the Darkness.** Henry Holt, 2001. ISBN 0-8050-6794-9. 149 pp. Intermediate–Middle school. Fiction, World.

This collection of Jewish stories is brought together through a fictional storyteller. Mara is a young woman being held in a Jewish death camp. Each night in the barracks, as a way of surviving, Mara tells her stories—some are humorous traditional tales, while others tell of miracles. These are stories drawn from deep fear but also from deep faith. Schmidt includes background notes on the stories' origins. TLC

2.31   Strangis, Joel. **Lewis Hayden and the War against Slavery.** Linnet, 1999. ISBN 0-208-02430-1. 167 pp. Middle school. Biography.

After escaping with his second wife and son from slavery, Lewis Hayden was behind the scenes in many efforts to put an end to slavery. In addition to many events not listed here, he assisted slaves journeying to freedom through the Underground Railroad, and he helped fund John Brown's raid on Harper's Ferry. After the Civil War, Hayden became a prominent politician and was instrumental in establishing a memorial for Crispus Attucks and the other four men murdered by the British at the beginning of the Revolutionary War. (Social Responsibility) PJ

3 Social Responsibility

Laura C. Jones and Tracy L. Coskie

As teachers we have many responsibilities. We are responsible for teaching our students. We are responsible for developing and implementing multiple curricula. We are responsible to the various local communities in which we work. We are responsible to our school administrations as well as to our local, state, and national professional organizations. And of course we are reminded of these myriad obligations on a daily basis. Yet we are rarely reminded of what could be described as one of our most critical responsibilities—fostering a sense of social responsibility in our selves and our students.

As Sheldon Berman describes it, social responsibility "focuses on the nature of a person's relationship with others and with the larger social and political world" (1997, p. 12). In other words, being socially responsible requires that our relationships with others take on an ethical dimension. To be socially responsible, we must take the other's perspective into account whenever we formulate new ideas or act on a new vision; we must listen carefully and compassionately; we must not only care for others, but must also do so within the framework of equity and justice.

For teachers this often seems like an insurmountable task. The question is asked: Just how might social responsibility be taught in schools? One place to begin developing this awareness of "otherness" is by bringing literature into the classroom. Through careful and compassionate readings of literature, students can begin to practice the necessary skills of "perspective-taking" and critical and reflective dialogue (Hansen-Krening, Mizokawa, & Wu, 2001). When teachers bring literature into the classroom, no matter what the grade level or content area, students naturally have the opportunity to explore other perspectives—to *listen* to the voices of the characters in the story, novel, or play.

We have put together this chapter as a way to help teachers explicitly address both the knowledge and skills involved in the concept of social responsibility. The books reviewed in this chapter offer the opportunity to address issues of social responsibility directly. These are books that provide models—of heroes and ordinary people alike. In both *Remix: Conversations with Immigrant Teenagers* (Budhos, 1999) and *Into a New Country: Eight Remarkable Women of the West* (Ketchum, 2000), for example, we hear from people who have had to reexamine their self-identities in light of changing social, economic, and geographic circumstances. The books in this chapter also provoke discussion. Consider the story of *A Special Fate: Chiune Sugihara, Hero of the Holocaust* (Gold, 2000). What are good decisions? And how do we make them?

Perhaps most important, these are books that present the perseverance of hope and of the interconnections of humankind. At the end of *A Special Fate,* the author writes that Sugihara wondered what kind of difference, if any, his actions had made: "Chiune had always felt that if he had even saved one refugee's life, it would have all been worth it" (Gold, 2000, p. 171). Decades after the war has ended, Sugihara learns that he had issued 6,000 Japanese transit visas. "An estimated 40,000 descendants of his visa recipients, now known as 'Sugihara Survivors,' are alive because of his extraordinary courage" (p. 175).

After Sugihara's death, the Japanese government erected a memorial: "The monument stands in a pond. The pond symbolizes humanity; the rings around the pond symbolize the widening ripple effect of an act of kindness" (Gold, 2000, p. 176). We believe the books annotated in this chapter can also serve as "ripples in the pond" of teaching social responsibility. And we hope that by including this section on social responsibility, we are taking one step forward in our work as socially responsible teachers. Our vision is of a world in which young people, when encountering such books together, can take their own steps forward toward social responsibility. Perhaps they too will be overcome with feelings of connectedness—and the ripple effect of social responsibility will widen.

References

Berman, S. (1997). *Children's social consciousness and the development of social responsibility.* Albany: State University of New York Press.

Hansen-Krening, N., Mizokawa, D. T., & Wu, Z. (2001). Literature: A driving force in ethnic identity and social responsibility development. In F. Salili & R. Hoosain (Eds.), *Multicultural education: Issues, policies, and practices* (pp. 211–23). Greenwich, CT: Information Age.

3.1   Ajmera, Maya, Olateju Omolodun, and Sarah Strunk. **Extraordinary Girls.** Charlesbridge, 1999. ISBN 0-88106-065-8. 47 pp. Elementary–Intermediate. Nonfiction, World.

The narrative introduces readers to girls who have already achieved success and recognition for their accomplishments, but it also emphasizes the importance of every girl working toward her own goals. The stories are inspirational not only because they describe girls who have made great achievements, but also because they show girls who have made a difference in their communities in various countries. This is a wonderful book for all, boys as well as girls, that highlights the extraordinary things girls do, the things they care about, and how they get involved in various activities and in their communities. (Informative and Educational Books; Visibility) MBC

3.2   Allison, Anthony. **Hear These Voices: Youth at the Edge of the Millennium.** Dutton, 1999. ISBN 0-525-4535-9. 170 pp. Middle school. Nonfiction, World.

This book truly does provide the voices of young people at the edge—at the edge of the millennium, the edge of society, and the edge of adulthood. But they should be at the center of our consciousness. These young people from all over the world have come face to face with some of the harshest realities of our world today, from AIDS and homelessness to prostitution and addiction. And they are emerging with a strong sense of self and a powerful belief in their own responsibility for working toward social justice. (Informative and Educational Books; Families, Friends, and Community) TLC

3.3   Ayres, Katherine. **Stealing South: A Story of the Underground Railroad.** Delacorte, 2001. ISBN 0-385-72912-X. 201 pp. Intermediate–Middle school. Fiction.

In this companion volume to *North by Night*, readers meet sixteen-year-old Will Spencer, who finds himself promising to rescue a runaway slave's brother and sister from their owner. While traveling south into Kentucky, Will meets southern plantation families who pose personal and moral issues for him to resolve. In the end, Will confronts his dilemmas and guides six young men, an elderly woman, and the runaway slave's sister to freedom. (Families, Friends, and Community) EMA

3.4   Belton, Sandra. **McKendree.** Greenwillow, 2000. ISBN 0-688-15950-8. 262 pp. Middle school. Realistic fiction, Ethnic specific.

"Tilara leaned closer, wondering at what she saw. Rich brown skin without one blemish. . . . Slowly, coming from deep within, a smile made its way across her face." This is just one powerful revelation of self that Tilara experiences during her summer vacation with Aunt Cloelle. Reading Tilara's coming-of-age story as she learns about first love, vibrant senior citizens, and, ultimately, self-acceptance is a rare treat. This is a must-read for all and an excellent book for a read-aloud or literature circles. (Visibility; Families, Friends, and Community) NHK

3.5   Blumberg, Rhoda. **Shipwrecked! The True Adventures of a Japanese Boy.** HarperCollins, 2001. ISBN 0-688-17484-1. 80 pp. Middle school. Nonfiction, Cross-cultural.

At age fourteen, Manjiro Nakahama became the first Japanese person to live in the United States. While fishing in 1841, Manjiro, later known as John Mung, was shipwrecked and marooned for six months before being rescued by a U.S. whaling ship. He was then educated in Massachusetts and later set off to participate in the gold rush. He soon earned enough money to return to Japan, narrowly avoided imprisonment and death, and ended up instructing the Japanese government about U.S. customs and policies. Woven throughout this nonfiction text are reproductions of mid-nineteenth-century Japanese artwork as well as sketches by Manjiro himself. (Informative and Educational Books) EMA

3.6   Bolden, Tonya. **Rock of Ages: A Tribute to the Black Church.** Illustrated by R. Gregory Christie. Alfred A. Knopf, 2001. ISBN 0-679-89485-3. Unpaged. Primary. Fiction, Ethnic specific.

Through poetically bold and lyrically spirited words, Tonya Bolden has made tribute to "her," the Black Church in America. Together with artist R. Gregory Christie, Bolden faithfully captures the presence and importance of the church throughout history, from the days of slavery to our present times. Highlighted within the congregation are the legendary figures who have contributed to the arts, politics, and sense of social responsibility of the African American community. This is a powerfully written book that provides informational resources as end pieces. (Families, Friends, and Community) EMA

3.7   Bridges, Ruby. **Through My Eyes.** Scholastic, 1999. ISBN 0-5901-8923-9. 64 pp. Primary. Nonfiction, Ethnic specific.

Ruby Bridges's recollections of her life as a courageous first grader helping to integrate the William Frantz Elementary

School in New Orleans in 1961 make for a powerful story of one young person's historical contribution to the civil rights movement. Throughout the narrative, Ruby Bridges maintains her point of view as a young girl while simultaneously documenting the historical account with newspaper articles and family interviews. (Visibility; Informative and Educational Books) EMA

Jane Addams Book Award, 2000

3.8 Budhos, Marina. **Remix: Conversations with Immigrant Teenagers.** Henry Holt, 1999. ISBN 0-8050-5113-9. 145 pp. Intermediate–Middle school. Nonfiction, Ethnic specific.

The dedication "To those teenagers who have arrived and those who have yet to arrive" sums up the power of this innovative collection of interviews of and writings by teenagers who have recently immigrated to the United States. Their stories are as varied as the teenagers themselves, and their narratives speak to the sometimes schizophrenic nature of being a teenage immigrant in the United States. (Informative and Educational Books; Visibility) LCJ

3.9 English, Karen. **Strawberry Moon.** Farrar, Straus and Giroux, 2001. ISBN 0-374-47122-3. 115 pp. Intermediate–Middle school. Fiction.

Through their long nighttime drive to visit Auntie Dot in Los Angeles, Imani and Blair's mother tells them stories of her childhood. They hear about what it was like for fifth grader Junie to leave her own mother in Chicago and move into Auntie Dot's house. Young readers will identify with Junie's trials and tribulations with friendships, fitting in, and dealing with family. Junie learns a lot that year about right and wrong—as well as about the power of love. TLC

3.10 Evans, Richard Paul. **The Tower: A Story of Humility.** Illustrated by Jonathan Linton. Simon & Schuster, 2001. ISBN 0-689-83467-5. Unpaged. Primary. Fiction, World.

The Tower is an incredibly powerful and insightful story about wisdom, humility, generosity, and life. Through one boy's efforts to make others look up to him, readers are reminded that being a great individual doesn't mean being higher than another, but instead lifting another higher. This story tells children who are familiar with competition, the importance of winning, and fame about what's truly important in life. Realistic watercolor illustrations are warm and touching. Although all characters in illustrations look Asian, neither culture nor ethnicity is specified. This is a good book for showing children that all human beings have issues in common regardless of race. (War and Resilience) IL

3.11   Gold, Alison Leslie. **A Special Fate: Chiune Sugihara, Hero of the Holocaust.** Scholastic, 2000. ISBN 0-590-39525-4. 176 pp. Middle school. Nonfiction, Cross-cultural.

Sugihara's story is seldom if ever told in history classes, yet his is an important story of courage and resilience. During World War II, Chiune Sugihara, a Japanese diplomat in Lithuania, defied his superior's orders to close the Japanese consulate and instead issued approximately 6,000 visas to Jews trying to escape the Nazis. Sugihara's courageous efforts saved thousands of lives. Middle school teachers in social studies or language arts classes would most certainly find this book a useful resource to supplement any discussion of World War II or the reading of *The Diary of Anne Frank.* Although Chiune Sugihara is no longer living, the author took great care to consult his family in researching and writing this work. (War and Resilience; Informative and Educational Books) LCJ

3.12   Hopkinson, Deborah. **A Band of Angels: A Story Inspired by the Jubilee Singers.** Illustrated by Raúl Colón. Atheneum, 1999. ISBN 0-6898-1062-8. Unpaged. Primary–Intermediate. Fiction, Cross-cultural.

This is the story of young Ella, a pianist, who helps the Fisk School's Jubilee Singers raise money to save the school and build Jubilee Hall. Although labeled as fiction, this story is based on the real life of Ella Sheppard Moore, who became the pianist for the Jubilee Singers, accompanied them on their concert tours, and helped raise enough money to build Fisk University's Jubilee Hall, the first permanent structure in the South for the education of Black students. (Visibility; Informative and Educational Books) EMA

Jane Addams Honor Book, 2000

3.13   Ketchum, Liza. **Into a New Country: Eight Remarkable Women of the West.** Little, Brown, 2000. ISBN 0-316-49597-2. 135 pp. Middle school. Nonfiction.

The narratives included in this work tell heretofore untold stories of the immigration to and development of the American West. The women's stories are as diverse and difficult as the conditions and terrains they had to surmount in order to "settle" in the western United States. Bethenia Owens-Adair, one of the voices finally heard, says, "I can never give up my freedom, my individuality" (p. 64). Each of the women portrayed in this work reflects this powerful determination and resolve to see her efforts come to fruition. (War and Resilience; Informative and Educational Books) LCJ

3.14   Krudop, Walter Lyon. **The Man Who Caught Fish.** Farrar, Straus and Giroux, 2000. ISBN 0-374-34786-7. Unpaged. Primary—Intermediate. Fiction.

Teachers looking for stories that explain the value of "sharing the wealth" rather than "winner takes all" will like this book. The pictures indicate that this story takes place in historical Thailand, but it is important to note that this is not a Thai folktale. This book would be a good read-aloud in the earlier grades as well as an appropriate text for any upper-elementary student. LCJ

3.15   Kudlinski, Kathleen. **Rosa Parks: Young Rebel.** Illustrated by Meryl Henderson. Aladdin, 2001. ISBN 0-689-83925-1. 224 pp. Intermediate. Nonfiction.

What an excellent book for students! History comes alive in this story of Rosa Parks as she grows from childhood to adulthood. Readers will enjoy learning about Parks's early years and relationships with family members, aspects of her life seldom covered in biographies of this historical figure. She was a fierce little girl who brooked no intimidation from White folks. Her courage in an era of fear and daily challenges for survival will inspire readers of all races. (War and Resilience) NHK

3.16   Lasky, Kathryn. **Vision of Beauty: The Story of Sarah Breedlove Walker.** Illustrated by Nneka Bennett. Candlewick, 2000. ISBN 0-7636-0253-1. 42 pp. Intermediate and up. Fiction, Cross-cultural.

Vision of Beauty is a beautifully written and illustrated biography of Sarah Breedlove Walker, an African American woman who became one of the richest women of her time. Madam Walker's early years of hard work and poor nutrition made her hair brittle and fall out. She created a special line of hair products that were especially well suited to African American women. As she grew increasingly successful, Madam Walker insisted on treating her employees well, and she also contributed financially to the improvement of the lives of African Americans. Madam Walker is an inspiration to women everywhere. (War and Resilience; Visibility) MBC

3.17 Littlesugar, Amy. **Freedom School, Yes!** Illustrated by Floyd Cooper. Philomel, 2001. ISBN 0-399-23006-8. Unpaged. Primary. Fiction, Ethnic specific.

Amy Littlesugar has written a fictional story based on the real-life Mississippi Freedom School Summer Project, which began in the summer of 1964. Told from the perspective of young Jolie, this story is set during the civil rights struggle when White volunteers from the North set up "freedom schools" for African American students in the South. Readers will become immersed in the tension of that time and witness vicariously the violence of the racists who burn down the Black church where the Freedom School is held. Through Floyd Cooper's masterful illustrations and Littlesugar's powerful narrative, readers will learn of the courage exhibited by the volunteers and the families housing teachers and by all who reached out to learn from one another. (War and Resilience) EMA

3.18 McBrier, Page. **Beatrice's Goat.** Illustrated by Lori Lohstoeter. Atheneum, 2001. ISBN 0-689-82460-2. Unpaged. Primary. Fiction, World.

Beatrice lives in an impoverished village in Uganda; through the auspices of the Heifer Project, her family is given a goat. This one little animal will bring food, security, and health to her family. The author presents this story with subtlety rather than didacticism, so readers won't feel preached to. Adults who want to instill a sense of global responsibility in young children can use this book as an introduction to issues of world hunger, helping others, and global responsibility. (Families, Friends, and Community) NHK

3.19 Mendelsohn, James. **Barbara Jordan: Getting Things Done.** Twenty-First Century, 2000. ISBN 0-7613-1467-9. 190 pp. Middle school. Biography.

Barbara Jordan will be remembered as one of our greatest citizens. At a time when it was neither easy to be a woman nor an African American in the political world, Barbara Jordan blazed a trail as a fierce fighter for justice and equity. Mendelsohn traces Jordan's life from her early struggles, through her political career, to her death at the early age of fifty-nine. Although she was intensely private about her personal life, readers will come away with a vivid picture of this political activist. (War and Resilience) NHK

3.20   Mollel, Tololwa M. **Song Bird.** Illustrated by Rosanne Litzinger. Clarion, 1999. ISBN 0-395-82908-9. 32 pp. Primary. Folktale, World.

In this lyrical adaptation of a Tanzanian folktale, Mollel tells a story of kindness and courage that begs to be read aloud. One day the people of Kung'ombe discover that all the cattle have disappeared. When Miriamu finds and saves a magic bird, together they rescue the cattle from the monster Makucha. In thanks, the people of Kung'ombe promise never to clear the Field of the Song Bird. Bright watercolors add a fanciful touch. An author's note provides the tale's origins, musical notations for the folk song, and a glossary of Swahili words. (Families, Friends, and Community) TLC

3.21   Myers, Walter Dean. **The Greatest: Muhammad Ali.** Scholastic, 2001. ISBN 0-590-54342-3. 172 pp. Intermediate–Middle school. Biography, Ethnic specific.

Award-winning author Walter Dean Myers triumphantly chronicles the life of the legendary boxer Muhammad Ali. In this page-turner, Myers captures the story of Cassius Clay's young life in the segregated 1950s in Louisville, Kentucky, through his world heavyweight championship victory over Sonny Liston, through Clay's transformation into Muhammad Ali. As students read about Ali's milestones, they also learn about the impact of politics, race, and religion on his life. (Informative and Educational Books) EMA

3.22   Myers, Walter Dean. **Malcolm X: A Fire Burning Brightly.** Illustrated by Leonard Jenkins. HarperCollins, 2000. ISBN 0-06-027707-6. Unpaged. Intermediate. Biography, Ethnic specific.

Malcolm X led a powerful, influential, and often misunderstood life. Myers masterfully reveals the story of Malcolm X and his great resilience in the face of adversity piled on adversity. One of the most important lessons to take from Malcolm X's life is his willingness to change his perspective and approach to life—from hatred to tolerance. (War and Resilience; Families, Friends, and Community) NHK

3.23   Myers, Walter Dean. **145th Street: Short Stories.** Delacorte, 2000. ISBN 0-385-32137-6. 151 pp. Middle school. Fiction, Ethnic specific.

Once readers have visited this neighborhood in Harlem, they're not likely to forget it. The people are the most memorable: Big Joe, who plans and carries out his own funeral party; Angela, who dreams of death; Billy, donning his boxing gloves in order to put food on the table; Kitty and Mack, too stubborn to let true love die. 145th Street is a place where terror, hunger, and desperation live—but so do laughter, respect, and hope. (War and Resilience; Families, Friends, and Community) TLC

3.24   Nolen, Jerdine. **Big Jabe.** Illustrated by Kadir Nelson. Lothrop, Lee & Shepard, 2000. ISBN 0-688-13662-1. Unpaged. Intermediate. Fiction, Ethnic specific.

This is a wonderful tall tale about a mysterious young man named Jabe who helps slaves escape using what seem to be magical powers and a pear tree. Jabe is plucked from the river by a young slave named Addy on the Plenty Plantation. After Addy finishes a delicious pear that Jabe gives her, they plant the seed on the riverbank. It grows into a huge tree with a mighty trunk. Life for the slaves dramatically improves after Jabe's arrival. When the overseer abuses a slave, the slave disappeares without a trace. Addy surmises that "Jabe took Pot-Tim to that pear tree." (Families, Friends, and Community) MBC

3.25   Rappaport, Doreen. **Freedom River.** Illustrated by Bryan Collier. Jump at the Sun/Hyperion, 2000. ISBN 0-7868-0350-9. Unpaged. Primary and up. Biography, Cross-cultural.

Freedom River is a compelling, narrowly focused biography about John Parker, a courageous former slave who worked the Underground Railroad to bring slaves to freedom and safety. Parker risked his life many times to help slaves escape to freedom, but this particular story relates a specific rescue in which he crept into the master's bedroom to whisk away a baby. The story is further enhanced by Bryan Collier's stunning illustrations. (War and Resilience) NHK

3.26   Ringgold, Faith. **If a Bus Could Talk: The Story of Rosa Parks.** Illustrated by Faith Ringgold. Simon & Schuster, 1999. ISBN 0-689-81892-0. Unpaged. Primary. Historical fiction, Ethnic specific.

Marcie hops on the bus, thinking it is her regular bus. Imagine her surprise when not only are the other passengers strangers, but also the bus itself can and does talk! Through this clever device, Ringgold tells the story of civil rights advocate Rosa Parks. As in all of her books, Ringgold provides pertinent information about important people and events in African American history, and she does it in such a way that readers and listeners will remember. The illustrations live up to the vivid artwork we've come to expect from Ringgold. (War and Resilience; Families, Friends, and Community) NHK

3.27   Rosen, Sybil. **Speed of Light.** Atheneum, 1999. ISBN 0-689-82437-8. 169 pp. Middle school. Fiction, Ethnic specific.

Speed of Light brings together two powerful historical events: the Jewish Holocaust of World War II and the civil rights movement. For eleven-year-old Audrey, these seem distant from life in 1950s Blue Gap, Virginia, until her father decides to help an African American, Mr. Cardwell, become a police officer. Suddenly old fears and distant hatreds become real. The family and their synagogue are attacked, and Audrey's live-in cousin, an Auschwitz survivor, is terrified. The Cardwells are in danger as well. Audrey's courage and convictions are lessons for us all. (Families, Friends, and Community) TLC

3.28   Ruffin, Frances E. **Martin Luther King, Jr. and the March on Washington.** Illustrated by Stephen Marchesi. Grosset & Dunlap, 2001. ISBN 0-448-42421-5. 48 pp. Primary. Biography.

All classrooms and school libraries should have this book. If the rest of the series is of equal quality and reading interest, they should get the series—All Aboard Reading—as well. We are fortunate that writers can make the lives, words, and thoughts of great folks accessible to our young children. Here, Martin Luther

King, Jr.'s life and words are presented in a lively and readable style. (War and Resilience) NHK

3.29   Ryan, Pam Muñoz. **Esperanza Rising.** Scholastic, 2000. ISBN 0-439-12041-1. 262 pp. Intermediate. Fiction.

"Did you know that when you lie down on the land, you can feel it breathe? That you can feel its heart beating?" This is a lesson Esperanza's father teaches her at the beginning of *Esperanza Rising* and a lesson that Esperanza has to relearn before the novel is finished. Esperanza and her family's lives are inseparable from the life of the earth as they travel from a rich plantation in the heart of Mexico to the difficult life in a farming labor camp in the southwestern portion of the United States. Despite their reduced circumstances, the family's hope continues to rise, as Esperanza's name implies. (Families, Friends, and Community; Informative and Educational Books) LCJ

3.30   Stewart, Gail B. **Teen Dropouts.** Photographs by Carl Franzén. Lucent, 1999. ISBN 1-56006-399-8. 112 pp. Middle school. Nonfiction.

This book, part of The Other America series, begins by providing the reader with the facts on teen dropouts—from who drops out to the complex set of circumstances under which they do so. Then the reader meets four dropouts who make these facts both real and immediate. Their stories are presented through pictures as well as their own words. The book concludes with ways the reader can get involved in helping students stay in school and recommendations for further reading. TLC

3.31   Vecchione, Patrice, editor. **Truth and Lies: An Anthology of Poems.** Henry Holt, 2001. ISBN 0-8050-6479-6. 142 pp. Middle school. Poetry, Ethnic specific and World.

As Vecchione explains in her introduction, "Poetry is a particular way of telling the truth." Perhaps that is why poetry seems such a good way to explore the ins and outs, ups and downs, and even the sideways of both truthfulness and falsehood. The collection includes a wide variety of American perspectives—including those of Linda Hogan, Julia Alvarez, and Janet S. Wong—as well as the views of poets from India, Spain, Poland, and other countries. Biographical notes and suggested readings are also provided. TLC

3.32　　Weidt, Maryann N. **Voice of Freedom: A Story about Frederick Douglass.** Illustrated by Jeni Reeves. Carolrhoda, 2001. ISBN 1-57505-553-8. 64 pp. Intermediate. Biography.

Weidt's book makes Douglass's powerful life story accessible to intermediate readers, telling of his escape from slavery and his dedication to free all slaves through his work as a writer and speaker. Douglass's energies extended to other social issues, including poverty and women's rights. Although Douglass was sometimes criticized for going beyond antislavery issues, his reply to such criticisms was, "I am not only an American slave, but a man, and as such, am bound to use my powers for the welfare of the whole human brotherhood." This book is one in the Creative Minds collection of biographies. (Informative and Educational Books) TLC

3.33　　Williams, Lori Aurelia. **Shayla's Double Brown Baby Blues.** Simon & Schuster, 2001. ISBN 0-689-82469-6. 300 pp. Middle school–High school. Fiction, Ethnic specific.

In this sequel to *When Kambia Elaine Flew in from Neptune,* the happy ending of that book is revisited. Shayla's best friend, Kambia, and her new friend, Lemm, are both tortured by their pasts. And Shayla's got her own troubles in the form of a baby half-sister and a recurring dream. Grandma Augustine tells her the dream is a sign that she is trying to discover what kind of woman she will become. It's not long before Shayla realizes that her daily decisions are a reflection of her future womanhood. (War and Resilience; Families, Friends, and Community) TLC

3.34　　Williams, Lori Aurelia. **When Kambia Elaine Flew in from Neptune.** Simon & Schuster, 2000. ISBN 0-689-82468-8. 246 pp. Middle school. Fiction, Ethnic specific.

Shayla's got troubles. As a result of fights with their mother, her sister Tia has run away. Shayla's mostly absent father has reappeared, and Grandma Augustine thinks it's time for Shayla to get religion. What's more, Shayla's strange new friend from next door is engaging in mysterious and frightening behaviors. This story is not for the fainthearted; it is as harrowing as it is healing. (War and Resilience) TLC

4 Families, Friends, and Community

Nancy Hansen-Krening and Michelle VanderVelde Woodfork

The books reviewed in this chapter open windows into the lives, loves, and tribulations of families, friends, and the communities surrounding those relationships. We witness folks who grapple with the complex issues surrounding interracial, intergenerational, and cross-cultural relationships, all topics of moment for our children. Though we may feel uneasy bringing them into our classrooms, every child is in the process of carving out a place in his or her family, circle of friends, and community. They are *learning how to be*. Therefore, books that touch on these issues should be read and discussed in the classroom.

The primary protagonist in *Beyond Mayfield* (Nelson, 1999), for example, a little girl, chooses to battle racism in her community. Another character in the book returns from battle in Vietnam only to face the quandary of determining his responsibility for fighting for civil rights in his own country. One character is African American and one is Western European American. Using stories such as this as a read-aloud or as shared readings in literature circles creates a natural approach to discussing the choices we face as individuals living in complex relationships. Each of the stories discussed in this chapter is "played out against the background of history and constructs a bridge for all of us through a shared concern with love, with . . . finding our places in our own families and communities" (Hansen-Krening, Mizokawa, & Wu, 2001).

Discussing and analyzing ways in which characters learn how to be, as well as observing how they resolve conflicts in relationships, lays bare our own approaches to problem solving. This in turn leads us to understand and respect other ways of living. Once readers are able to empathize with and value diverse perspectives, the scope of their social web is broadened. Stories, then, that unveil characters and their methods of working through relationships—whether interracial, intergenerational, or cross-cultural—are natural springboards to developing empathy, valuing diverse perspectives, and taking action by become socially responsible.

Reference

Hansen-Krening, N., Mizokawa, D. T., & Wu, Z. (2001). Literature: A driving force in ethnic identity and social responsibility development. In F. Salili & R. Hoosain (Eds.), *Multicultural education: Issues, policies, and practices* (pp. 211–23). Greenwich, CT: Information Age.

———

4.1 Allen, Debbie. **Brothers of the Knight.** Illustrated by Kadir Nelson. Dial, 1999. ISBN 0-8037-2488-8. Unpaged. Primary. Folktale, Ethnic specific.

A housekeeper who understands twelve boys rekindles love and understanding between the youngsters and their father living in Harlem. Readers will enjoy the rhythms of English and the clever retelling of the fairy tale "The Twelve Dancing Princesses." (Visibility) IL

4.2 Altman, Linda Jacobs. **The Legend of Freedom Hill.** Illustrated by Cornelius Van Wright & Ying-Hwa Hu. Lee & Low, 2000. ISBN 1-58430-003-5. Unpaged. Primary–Adult. Fiction.

The story in this extraordinary picture book takes place in the social climate of the 1850s in the American West, focusing particularly on California's cultural and ethnic history. Two girls, one African American and the other Jewish, discover the reality of racism in their own community when the African American girl's mother is taken away by a slave catcher. The girls take immediate action, revealing the depth of their friendship and level of bravery. (War and Resilience; Social Responsibility) MVW

4.3 Battle-Lavert, Gwendolyn. **The Music in Derrick's Heart.** Illustrated by Colin Bootman. Holiday House, 2000. ISBN 0-8234-1353-5. Unpaged. Primary. Fiction.

Follow Derrick's experience of learning how to play the harmonica from his Uncle Booker T in this lovely picture book. When Derrick discovers the secret of playing the harmonica from his heart, he continues a family tradition that allows all members of his family to continue enjoying harmonica music. MVW

4.4 Bennett, James W. **Blue Star Rapture.** Aladdin, 2001. ISBN 0-689-84150-7. 197 pp. Intermediate–Adult. Fiction.

Blue Star Rapture traces a young boy's inner journey as he begins to think about the motivations behind his actions and the decisions he makes in life. His best friend's ability to play basketball seems to be a great way to gain personal attention and fame, until certain events occur and specific people come into the boy's life that cause him to experience disequilibrium. This is a great story about a boy who is starting to question his character, morality, and the ethics behind his actions. The book contains some profanity and mature themes. MVW

4.5 Bercaw, Edna Coe. **Halmoni's Day.** Illustrated by Robert Hunt. Dial, 2000. ISBN 0-8037-2444-6. Unpaged. Primary. Fiction, Ethnic specific.

This is a powerful story about love and bonding between a Korean American girl, Jennifer, and her grandmother, who is from Korea. The language barrier and Halmoni's (Grandma's) differences from Jennifer's friends' grandmas do not prevent Jennifer and Halmoni's understanding and acceptance of each other. Lovely, warm illustrations catch features of authentic Korean clothing and Korean dishes on a dinner table. (Surprisingly, the illustrator is not Korean.) As in so many books with Korean characters, the Korean War is an unnecessary issue in this story. (Visibility) IL

4.6 Bierhorst, John. **Is My Friend at Home? Pueblo Fireside Tales.** Illustrated by Wendy Watson. Farrar, Straus and Giroux, 2001. ISBN 0-374-33550-8. Unpaged. Primary. Folktale, Cross-cultural.

In his retellings of seven Pueblo trickster tales, Bierhorst celebrates friendship. Each short story shows friends in a different light: helpful, mischievous, smart, and even dangerous. The stories also explore the natural world. Why are peaches sweet? How did coyote get such short ears? Children will enjoy the lessons, the storyteller rhythm, and the cartoonlike illustrations of the animal friends. TLC

4.7 Bierhorst, John. **The People with Five Fingers: A Native Californian Creation Tale.** Illustrated by Robert Andrew Parker. Marshall Cavendish, 2000. ISBN 0-7614-5058-0. 28 pp. Primary. Folktale, Cross-cultural.

Coyote makes his wishes, puts on his belt, and says, "What I plan will stand true." This cross-cultural creation tale, told throughout the California Indian nations, is shared with readers in few words supported by watercolor illustrations. Coyote, together with the Gopher brothers, Lizard, and other friends, creates a world of clear rivers and valleys. Then they fill the world with people who are many colors and speak many different languages. As the author claims, "Accomplished storytellers, native Californians were also gifted as prophets." TLC

4.8   Bruchac, Joseph. **Bowman's Store: A Journey to Myself.** Lee & Low, 2001. ISBN 1-58430-027-2. 315 pp. Intermediate–Middle school. Autobiography, Ethnic specific.

In this memoir of growing up with his grandparents, Bruchac lovingly weaves together Native American tales and family stories. Bruchac's own life story brings together themes that most young adults can identify with—struggling to know oneself, meeting death, first love, and learning to connect with the world. Each chapter is a complete vignette, but all are enriched as themes are revisited in the circular narrative by this consummate storyteller. Black-and-white family photos make the people and place real, encouraging the reader to identify with Bruchac's story. (Visibility) TLC

4.9   Bryan, Ashley, editor. **Ashley Bryan's ABC of African American Poetry.** Illustrated by Ashley Bryan. Aladdin, 2001. ISBN 0-689-84045-4. 27 pp. All grades. Poetry.

As Bryan states in the introduction, this book is much more than an ABC book. He has brought together a multitude of African American poets by taking the first lines from some of their works in order to create a book that represents the variety of voices and stories that are part of the African American experience. Bryan's vivid illustrations add to the flowing nature of this unique text. (Informative and Educational Books) LCJ

4.10   Bunting, Eve. **Jin Woo.** Illustrated by Chris K. Soentpiet. Clarion, 2001. ISBN 0-395-93872-4. 32 pp. Primary. Fiction, Cross-cultural.

Eve Bunting has attempted to weave the complexity of three emotional themes into her story of Jin Woo: accepting a new sibling, adoption, and interracial families. Young David is about to become a big brother, but he is happily settled in his family of three and isn't sure how to feel about the baby brother who is about to arrive. Not only does David have to deal with a younger sibling, but he also has to grapple with the fact that this new brother is being adopted from Korea. Underlying these emotions are the realities of learning and understanding cultural differences in the newly formed interracial family. The story raises its many issues a bit too quickly as Mom and Dad help David realize the love he has for his new sibling. EMA

4.11   Cameron, Ann. **Gloria's Way.** Illustrated by Lis Toft. Frances Foster Books, 2000. ISBN 0-374-32670-3. 96 pp. Intermediate. Fiction.

This delightful collection of fictional stories is about a young girl named Gloria who is grappling with many of the common issues of childhood. Cameron does an excellent job of creating characters who deal with very real issues such as the ethics of keeping promises, the demands that work sometimes puts on parents and families, and the adventures that having a pet can bring. All of the stories in this book are both entertaining and rich with description and plot development. (Visibility) LCJ

4.12   Cheng, Andrea. **Grandfather Counts.** Illustrated by Ange Zhang. Lee & Low, 2000. ISBN 1-58430-010-8. Unpaged. Intermediate. Fiction.

Grandfather Counts is the story of a biracial girl, Helen, who meets her Chinese grandfather for the first time. At first grandfather is reluctant to interact with Helen, but then the two discover their mutual love of trains. Grandfather teaches Helen to count to ten in Chinese, and he learns to count to ten in English. They begin teaching each other more words, and soon a special bond begins. MBC

4.13   Cooke, Trish. **The Grandad Tree.** Illustrated by Sharon Wilson. Candlewick, 2000. ISBN 0-7636-0815-7. Unpaged. Primary. Fiction, Ethnic specific.

Young Leigh and her big brother Vin plant a seed by the apple tree in memory of their grandfather. Vin helps his younger sister remember their grandfather playing with them under that tree, and they recall the tales he told of growing up and raising a family. Over time they watch the seasons change—how, over time, life comes to an end. "That's life," their granddad used to say. Both Leigh and Vin know that things will grow and change, but they'll always have their love for their granddad. This affectionate story is softly complemented with the gentle illustrations of Sharon Wilson. EMA

4.14   Coy, John. **Strong to the Hoop.** Illustrated by Leslie Jean-Bart. Lee & Low, 2000. ISBN 1-880000-80-6. 32 pp. Intermediate. Fiction.

Any young boy who has a passion for basketball will enjoy this story. In this rite-of-passage tale, James finally gets the opportunity to move from the sidelines to the center court of his favorite sport. With realistic dialogue and a unique presentation of the text, *Strong to the Hoop* makes for an enjoyable read. (Visibility) LCJ

4.15   Draper, Sharon M. **Romiette and Julio.** Atheneum, 1999. ISBN 0-689-82180-8. 236 pp. Middle school. Fiction.

When Romiette's best friend, Destiny, tells her that her horoscope predicts a new man coming into her life, neither has any idea what fate has in store. Romiette (a.k.a. Afroqueen) meets Julio (a.k.a. Spanishlover) in an Internet chat room—only to discover that they go to the same high school. Real trouble hits when the Devildogs, a new gang at school, decide they disapprove of the couple's interracial relationship. Unlike Shakespeare's *Romeo and Juliet*, a happy ending is in the stars for this young couple. Regardless of its literary merit, young people are sure to enjoy this modern romantic adventure. TLC

4.16   Fishman, Cathy Goldberg. **On Shabbat.** Illustrated by Melanie W. Hall. Atheneum, 2001. ISBN 0-689-83894-8. Unpaged. Primary. Fiction, Ethnic specific.

Fishman invites her readers into the home of a contemporary family as they celebrate the weekly Jewish holiday of Shabbat. When all is prepared (work week items put away, table set, and candles lit), the Shabbat Queen is invited into the house. During this time of renewal, the family attends synagogue, plays games, and studies the Torah. Soon it is time to make Havdalah—to end Shabbat and begin a new week. A glossary of the Yiddish and Hebrew words is provided, and Hall's illustrations are both peaceful and warm. TLC

4.17   Freschet, Gina. **Beto and the Bone Dance.** Farrar, Straus and Giroux, 2001. ISBN 0-374-31720-8. Unpaged. Primary. Fiction.

Beto is excited about celebrating *el Dia de los Muertos*—the Day of the Dead. He wants to put something special on the altar to honor his recently departed grandmother, but what can he choose? When Beto falls asleep during the family's visit to the cemetery, the answer comes to him in a dream. Freschet's vibrant paintings and appealing story enliven themes that many children will find familiar. (Bilingual and Multilingual Literature) TLC

4.18 Gilles, Almira Astudillo. **Willie Wins.** Illustrated by Carl Angel. Lee & Low, 2001. ISBN 1-58430-023-X. Unpaged. Primary–Adult. Fiction.

A young boy struggles to find an effective way to respond to a school bully. Then an ordinary school project becomes an extraordinary experience for Willie and his friends when his father shares a rare family treasure. Willie learns lessons about his father's love, friendship, and taking pride in his family's Filipino history in this sweet and colorful picture book. MVW

4.19 Grimes, Nikki. **Is It Far to Zanzibar? Poems about Tanzania.** Illustrated by Betsey Lewin. Lothrop, Lee & Shepard, 2000. ISBN 0-688-13157-3. Unpaged. Primary. Poetry, Ethnic specific.

This delightful collection of poetry developed from Grimes's visit to Tanzania. The poems are playful and give the reader the feel of being on holiday as they depict bus rides, market scenes, family visits, landscapes, and exciting adventures. The Swahili language is woven throughout, and a glossary and map are provided at the end of the book. Lewin's fun watercolors complement the poems nicely. (Visibility) EMA

4.20 Grimes, Nikki. **My Man Blue.** Illustrated by Jerome Lagarrigue. Dial, 1999. ISBN 0-8037-2326-1. 32 pp. Primary–Intermediate. Poetry, Ethnic specific.

Grimes has composed a collection of poems centered on the friendship between Damon, a young African American boy, and Blue, a friend of Damon's mother. Blue has just lost his father and is now the man of the house. Blue was a father who once had a son and vows never to lose another to the streets. Damon and Blue become each other's guiding strength as Blue reaches out: "His hands are strong stories. He tells them sometimes when I let him hold mine." The story of their relationship is told with great sensitivity. EMA

4.21   Grimes, Nikki. **A Pocketful of Poems.** Illustrated by Javaka Steptoe. Clarion, 2001. ISBN 0-395-93868-6. 30 pp. Primary. Poetry, Ethnic specific.

Nikki Grimes has creatively and joyfully composed a magnificent wordplay book. Grimes's poems, together with Javaka Steptoe's colorful collages, present young Tiana, who has a pocket full of words. Text and illustration visually explode with words such as *Spring, Hot,* and *Homer*—a summer word, another warm word, and a word shaped like a bat! Each double-spread is filled with city scenes of dancing words and paired poems, one in free verse and one in haiku. This book of poetry and art will tantalize young readers and poets who love to play with words. (Visibility) EMA

4.22   Hamilton, Virginia. **Bluish.** Blue Sky, 1999. ISBN 0-590-28879-2. 127 pp. Intermediate–Middle school. Fiction, Ethnic specific.

Dreenie is the new girl in fifth grade. Right away Tulie, an insecure biracial classmate who pretends she is Spanish, latches on. But it's Natalie, the girl in the wheelchair, whom Dreenie can't stop thinking about. Natalie's mother thinks the kids call her "Blewish" because her father is Black and her mother Jewish. Dreenie thinks, "Bluish fits her. This girl is like moonlight. So pale you see the blue veins all over." The unusual style and pacing of the narrative add tension to this poignant story of need, friendship, and hope. TLC

4.23   Heo, Yumi. **One Sunday Morning.** Illustrated by Yumi Heo. Orchard, 1999. ISBN 0-531-30156-7. Unpaged. Primary. Fiction, Ethnic specific.

An afternoon in the park with Dad! What a perfect day, complete with enchanting sounds of fun and play. Bike riding: "Whoosh"; remote-control boats: "Whirr, whirr"; and sodas to cool off: "plop, blubba, blubba." The fun comes to an end all to soon as Minho's father pulls up the blind—"Wheep"—and Minho cries, "Oh no! It was only a Dreeeeeeeeeeam." Korean American Yumi Heo writes joyfully of a day in the park. This colorful book is filled with the action and movement of childlike drawings and onomatopoeic words. This is a companion book to *One After-noon*, in which Minho spends the day in the city with his mother. EMA

4.24 Hubbell, Patricia. **City Kids.** Illustrated by Teresa Flavin. Marshall Cavendish, 2001. ISBN 0-7614-5079-3. 32 pp. Primary and up. Poetry.

In this collection of poems about kids living in the city, readers will find descriptions of the people and the sights and sounds commonly found in busy city neighborhoods. The author includes some less glamorous urban topics such as muggings, graffiti, and homelessness, so the text includes an element of realism that younger readers and listeners may find disturbing. (Visibility) MBC

4.25 Jiménez, Francisco. **Breaking Through.** Houghton Mifflin, 2001. ISBN 0-618-01173-0. 195 pp. Intermediate–Middle school. Autobiography, Ethnic specific.

Breaking Through is Jiménez's autobiographical sequel to his award-winning book *The Circuit*. This book covers his teenage years in the 1950s and 1960s, beginning with his family's deportation back to Mexico. In simple but powerful language, Jiménez depicts the family's struggle to make ends meet through long hours of labor, as well as his own challenges in making his way through school. Young readers will be particularly drawn to the author's description of his relationships with his older brother, Roberto, and with his bitter father. (War and Resilience) TLC

4.26 Johnson, Angela. **Down the Winding Road.** Illustrated by Shane Evans. DK Ink, 2000. ISBN 0-7894-2596-3. Unpaged. Primary. Fiction, Ethnic specific.

Trust Angela Johnson to tell stories that touch the heart and connect with readers of all ethnicities. The children in this story accompany their parents on a visit to the Old Ones, the family members who carry the family history. As the children swing, walk, listen, and talk, they express their love and respect for these accepting, vital Old Ones. The illustrations infuse the story with additional warmth and affection. (Visibility) NHK

4.27　Johnson, Dinah. **Quinnie Blue.** Illustrated by James Ransome. Henry Holt, 2000. ISBN 0-8050-4378-0. Unpaged. Primary–Adult. Fiction.

A young girl wonders about the life of the woman she is named after—Quinnie Blue, her grandmother. In this gorgeous picture book written in vivacious language, both past and present are captured as a young girl tries to imagine the similarities between herself and her beloved grandmother. MVW

4.28　Johnson, Dolores. **My Mom Is My Show-and-Tell.** Illustrated by Dolores Johnson. Marshall Cavendish, 1999. ISBN 0-7614-5041-6. Unpaged. Primary. Fiction, Ethnic specific.

Can David's mother handle being his show-and-tell at school? David reminds his mother, "Don't tell any of your long stories. Talk up real loud, but don't shout. And whatever happens, under no circumstance, don't you dare call me Pumpkin." This is a heartwarming, humorous story about a mother-son relationship. DH & DB

4.29　Kurtz, Jane. **Faraway Home.** Illustrated by E. B. Lewis. Harcourt, 2000. ISBN 0-15-200036-4. Unpaged. Primary–Intermediate. Fiction, World.

As Desta's father prepares for a trip back to Ethiopia, his homeland, Desta is full of questions yet begins to worry: "Ethiopia is so far away. I don't want you to go." Desta's father carefully recounts his childhood in his small village in Ethiopia. This poignant story offers the reader an excellent contrast between life in the father's faraway land and Desta's own world. The watercolor illustrations convey the true meaning of home. (Informative and Educational Books) DH & DB

4.30　Lester, Julius. **What a Truly Cool World.** Illustrated by Joe Cepeda. Scholastic, 1999. ISBN 0-590-86468-8. Unpaged. Primary–Intermediate. Fiction, Ethnic specific.

Whether teachers use this book in schools will depend on the nature of the school community because the story is about a Christian God. *What a Truly Cool World* is the story of how God created butterflies. The language has a slight flavor of southern Black English, and God and his main angels are definitely Black. What a story! Readers and listeners of all ages will be caught up in the vitality and energy of Lester's story and Cepeda's illustrations. NHK

4.31 Lewis, Rose. **I Love You Like Crazy Cakes.** Illustrated by Jane Dyer. Little, Brown, 2000. ISBN 0-316-52538-3. Unpaged. Primary. Fiction.

The rich, gentle watercolor images by Jane Dyer give life to this sentimental, emotional story of adoption. Journalist Rose Lewis shares a mother's love as she narrates her trip to China to adopt a baby girl. Lewis captures the emotions of the adoptive American mother as well as those of the Chinese birth mother with her final words: "The tears were for your Chinese mother. . . . I wanted her to know that we would always remember her, . . . and I hoped somehow she knew you were safe and happy in the world." EMA

4.32 Look, Lenore. **Henry's First-Moon Birthday.** Illustrated by Yumi Heo. Atheneum, 2001. ISBN 0-689-82294-4. Unpaged. Primary. Fiction, Ethnic specific.

This is an entertaining story about a little Chinese American girl who helps her grandmother prepare for the traditional Chinese birthday party for her one-month-old brother (first-moon birthday). Interesting information about Chinese traditions and foods, as well as Chinese words, are woven into the story naturally. Children will be intrigued by the charming story and illustrations. A helpful glossary of Chinese words and terms is provided on the first page. IL

4.33 Madrigal, Antonio Hernández. **Blanca's Feather.** Illustrated by Gerardo Suzán. Rising Moon, 2000. ISBN 0-87358-743-X. Unpaged. Primary. Fiction.

In this heartwarming story about a girl and her pet hen, Madrigal weaves together the rituals of the Feast of St. Francis of Assisi ceremony with the special friendship between Rosalía and her pet hen, Blanca. When Rosalía cannot locate Blanca in time for the annual blessing, she finds a way around the problem and receives a surprise. Suzán's creative scenes infuse this story with a whimsical element of fantasy. The author's note provides an excellent explanation of and background for the Feast of St. Francis, which is celebrated in Mexico and many other countries, including the United States. DH & DB

4.34   Madrigal, Antonio Hernández. **Erandi's Braids.** Illustrated by
Tomie dePaola. Putnam's, 1999. ISBN 0-399-23212-5. Unpaged.
Primary. Fiction, Ethnic specific.

Soon it will be Erandi's birthday. She can hardly wait to go to the
square to select her gift with her mama. She has her eyes set on a
yellow party dress for the fiesta and a doll wearing the same
beautiful yellow dress. She knows she can't have both. She also
knows her mother needs a new fishing net. Through the warmth
of Madrigal's story line and dePaola's folklike characters, readers will find themselves looking deep into the loving eyes shared
by mother and daughter as Erandi selflessly and courageously
gives up her hair to help her mother buy a new fishing net and to
celebrate her own birthday with a new dress and doll. EMA

4.35   Monk, Isabell. **Family.** Illustrated by Janice Lee Porter. Carolrhoda, 2001. ISBN 1-57505-485-X. Unpaged. Primary. Fiction.

Early elementary teachers looking for books that represent
both the universal and the unique characteristics of families
will find this is an excellent book to add to their professional
collection. Hope's Aunt Poogee has called the relatives together
for a family reunion. The story reflects the cultural and ethnic
diversity that can exist in one family, as well as the familial
bonds of love that tie family members together. Recipes are
included at the end of the book so that readers can make any or
all of the dishes that the individual family members bring to
the reunion dinner. LCJ

4.36   Mora, Pat. **The Rainbow Tulip.** Illustrated by Elizabeth Sayles.
Viking, 1999. ISBN 0-670-87291-1. Unpaged. Primary. Fiction.

"It is hard to be different. It is sweet and sour, like lime sherbet."
Stella, a first-grader, knows her Mexican heritage sets her apart
from her schoolmates. In this touching story, a Mexican American girl experiences the difficulties and pleasures of being different when she wears a tulip costume in all the colors of the
rainbow for the school May Day parade. The text's natural
code-switching between Spanish and English, combined with
watercolor paintings, make this a warm and entertaining story
that celebrates diversity. (Note: The word *tuipán* is misspelled—
it should be *tulipán*.) (Bilingual and Multilingual Literature) DH
& DB

4.37   Myers, Walter Dean. **The Blues of Flats Brown.** Illustrated by Nina Laden. Holiday House, 2000. ISBN 0-8234-1480-9. Unpaged. Intermediate. Fiction, Ethnic specific.

This is the story of two hound dogs, Flats Brown and Caleb, who escape their mean owner to embark on musical careers. Eventually their owner catches up with them, and they must move on. The dogs earn fame and fortune but still live in fear of their owner finding them. When the dreaded moment arrives, Flats Brown melts a hostile heart with his soulful song about a mean dog owner who just wants to be loved. MBC

4.38   Na, An. **A Step from Heaven.** Front Street, 2001. ISBN 1-886910-58-8. 156 pp. Middle school–High school. Fiction, Ethnic specific.

This story of a new immigrant family from Korea reflects the hardship of living as a newcomer and non-English speaker in the United States. The father becomes abusive, and the rest of the family suffers. Some chapters are written in short sentences that sound like poetry. Although some Korean words are used with no translation, they are understandable in context. Despite these Korean words, Korean culture itself does not specifically stand out. Readers should be able to extrapolate from this story the difficulty *all* newcomers experience in a new land, not just Korean Americans. (Note: One word is used incorrectly: younger brother Joon calls his older sister Young *uhn-nee,* which designates the name used by a younger sister for an older sister. Younger brother's word for an older sister is *nhu-na.*) (Visibility) IL

4.39   Namioka, Lensey. **Yang the Eldest and His Odd Jobs.** Illustrated by Kees de Kiefte. Little, Brown, 2000. ISBN 0-316-59011-8. 121 pp. Intermediate. Fiction, Ethnic specific.

Lensey Namioka engages readers once again in the lives of the Yang family. This series' fourth book is centered on talented First Brother and his need for a new violin. The story is told with empathy and humor through the voice of Third Sister, who shares her brother's moneymaking adventures, from babysitting to fiddling at the street fair. She is also the one who keeps him in line as he wanders and learns about life as a teenager. Woven throughout the story are insights into this close-knit immigrant family's cultural traditions and values. Readers learn that in China, the government supports talented musicians so that students like Yang don't have to purchase their own instruments or pay for lessons. As in all the stories about the Yangs, it is the family members' love for one another and the power of music that binds them and gives them strength and perseverance. EMA

4.40   Nelson, Vaunda Micheaux. **Beyond Mayfield.** Putnam's, 1999. ISBN 0-399-23355-5. 138 pp. Intermediate–Adult. Fiction.

Set in the 1960s, *Beyond Mayfield* is narrated by a young African American girl who shares the lessons she learns about prejudice, both her own and that of others toward her. Meg's integrated neighborhood experience has provided her with a unique perspective about race in the United States. At school she is confronted with racism from both peers and adults. Readers will gain insight into the civil rights struggle through both Meg's experiences and those of one young European American war veteran who risks his life to ally with African Americans in the Deep South. This is an excellent book for prompting discussion about the prejudice, discrimination, interracial relationships, and power and privilege that are deeply rooted in the history of the United States. (War and Resilience; Social Responsibility) MVW

4.41   Nye, Naomi Shihab, editor. **Salting the Ocean: 100 Poems by Young Poets.** Illustrated by Ashley Bryan. Greenwillow, 2000. ISBN 0-688-16193-6. 112 pp. Intermediate. Poetry.

"Brenda erases the last line of her poem about her grandmother many times before turning the poem in. 'I think I got it,' she says. And I didn't know what it was—when I started writing. I had to find it," says Naomi Shihab Nye, the editor of this amazing collection of poetry written by children in grades 1 through 12. The collection is accompanied by stunning illustrations from Ashley Bryan, whose résumé includes several Coretta Scott King honor book awards. Because students enjoy reading and find inspiration in poetry by their peers, this is a necessary book for every classroom. MBC

4.42   Pak, Soyung. **Dear Juno.** Illustrated by Susan Kathleen Hartung. Viking, 1999. ISBN 0-670-88252-6. Unpaged. Primary. Fiction, Ethnic specific.

Although Juno cannot read Korean, the language his grandma in Korea has used to write him a letter, he can still communicate with her. He knows what the photograph and dried flowers enclosed in the letter mean, and he decides to write her back. The love between grandmother and grandson is clear and will touch readers of all ages. Some adults may be offended by illustrations that stereotype the Asian characters with small and slightly slanted black eyes. (Visibility) IL

4.43   Park, Linda Sue. **A Single Shard.** Clarion, 2001. ISBN 0-395-97827-0. 152 pp. Intermediate–Middle school. Historical fiction, World.

Linda Sue Park reaches back to twelfth-century Korea to craft a story of a young orphan boy's perseverance and creativity. In the potters' village of Ch'ul'po, Crane-man raises a ten-year-old orphan named Tree Ear, a name that is significant because it is a "name for a mushroom that grows without the benefit of a parent-seed." Crane-man and Tree Ear live under a bridge, but Tree Ear is drawn to the village potters' artistry, especially that of Min. Eventually, Tree Ear becomes an apprentice to Min and must deliver two vases to the palace in the hopes of receiving a royal commission. His journey to the palace meets with disaster, and he has only a single shard to show. As a backdrop to the story, Park shares useful information about the culture and conditions of twelfth-century Korea. EMA

4.44   Partridge, Elizabeth. **Oranges on Golden Mountain.** Illustrated by Aki Sogabe. Dutton, 2001. ISBN 0-525-46453-0. Unpaged. Primary. Fiction, Cross-cultural.

This picture book tells the story of Jo Lee, a young Chinese immigrant who leaves his village in China during the 1850s to travel to the United States. Drought has stricken his village, so his mother sends him to California to work with his uncle in a fishing village. The reluctant boy journeys across the ocean, learning to cope with his homesickness. He protects his mother's orange cuttings and plants them, along with himself, in his new country. He finds further comfort in her promise that "he is never alone. His dream spirit, his Hun, will make sure of that." The story ends with the boy's Hun reconnecting him with his family. With assistance, young readers and listeners will be introduced to a historical period of Chinese immigration. EMA

4.45   Philip, Neil, editor. **Weave Little Stars into My Sleep: Native American Lullabies.** Photographs by Edward S. Curtis. Clarion, 2001. ISBN 0-618-08856-3. Unpaged. Primary and up. Nonfiction.

Philip has collected a variety of lullabies, from the simple words of the Arapaho "Go to sleep, Baby dear, Go to sleep, Baby" to the highly poetic Acoma "Cloud-Cradle" song; from the teasing of the Hopi "Owl Kachina Song" to the tenderness of the Inuit "Mother's Song." The lullabies are accompanied by Curtis's photographs of Native American women and children. At the end, Philip includes important information about his collecting process as well as acknowledgments for both text and photos. (Informative and Educational Books; Social Responsibility) TLC

4.46   Pinkney, Brian. **Cosmo and the Robot.** Illustrated by Brian Pinkney. Greenwillow, 2000. ISBN 0-688-15941-9. Unpaged. Primary. Fiction.

Cosmo's best friend is no ordinary friend—he is a gentle robot. But one day Rex bumps his head, begins acting like a monster, and needs to be taken to the asteroid dump. At this point, Cosmo knows that life on Mars will never be the same. When Cosmo's parents give him a Solar System Utility belt, he realizes that his luck is going to change and that anything is possible. DH & DB

4.47   Rohmer, Harriet, editor. **Honoring Our Ancestors: Stories and Pictures by Fourteen Artists.** Children's Book Press, 1999. ISBN 0-89239-158-8. 31 pp. Primary–Adult. Nonfiction.

This treasure of a book brings together fourteen artists and illustrators to express their respective ancestral and ethnic pride, from Arab American to Chinese, Pacific Islander to West Indian. It also pays tribute to influential people from diverse backgrounds who are unlikely to be discussed in history books. This text will inspire children and adults alike to consider their own family histories. MVW

4.48   Rosales, Melodye. **Minnie Saves the Day.** Little, Brown, 2001. ISBN 0-316-75605-9. 84 pp. Intermediate. Fiction.

Although the main story is about Minnie, a brown rag doll, and her new owner, Hester Merriweather, the reader can't help but learn more about the African American experience during the

1930s. The story revolves around Hester and Minnie, who help solve a problem for Mama. The afterword, titled "Chocolate-Covered Memories," contains historical information on subjects such as the Great Migration, the entertainment industry, and even how difficult it was to find African American dolls during that period; the afterword is one of the best features of the book. (Informative and Educational Books; Social Responsibility) MBC

4.49 Rosen, Michael J. **Chanukah Lights Everywhere.** Illustrated by Melissa Iwai. Harcourt, 2001. ISBN 0-15-202447-6. Unpaged. Primary. Fiction, Ethnic specific.

Rosen has created a counting book that celebrates Hanukkah as the Festival of Lights. A young boy looks around him to identify the same number of lights as there are candles on the menorah each night. Young children will enjoy counting the number of cats on each spread of the illustrations—they too match the number of menorah candles. The end of the book includes a historical note on the significance of this Jewish celebration. TLC

4.50 Rosen, Michael J. **Our Eight Nights of Hanukkah.** Illustrated by DyAnne DiSalvo-Ryan. Holiday House, 2000. ISBN 0-8234-1476-0. Unpaged. Primary. Fiction, Ethnic specific.

The book presents one little Jewish child's experience of the eight days of Hanukkah. In addition to providing readers with information about Hanukkah, this book attempts to share Hanukkah spirits with the less fortunate and with people of different religions. Because of this inclusive approach, the text could have been improved if it had included information about holidays other than Hanukkah and Christmas. The illustrations are heartwarming, and a helpful note about pronouncing Hebrew words is provided. IL

4.51 Sanders, Scott Russell. **A Place Called Freedom.** Illustrated by Thomas B. Allen. Aladdin, 2001. ISBN 0-689-84001-2. 28 pp. Primary–Intermediate. Fiction, Ethnic specific.

Although this picture book is based on actual events before the Civil War, it is the fictional account of how one family of newly freed slaves moved north from Tennessee and over the years created a thriving African American community in Indiana. "Again and again Papa went back to Tennessee, and each time he came home with more of the folks we loved." This story is instructive about African American migration and Indiana history, as well as an empowering narrative of African American determination and self-reliance. (War and Resilience) MVW

4.52   San Souci, Robert D., reteller. **Callie Ann and Mistah Bear.** Illustrated by Don Daily. Dial, 2000. ISBN 0-8037-1766-0. Unpaged. Primary. Fiction.

In this story based on Alcée Fortier's *Louisiana Folk-tales* and Joel Chandler Harris's *Daddy Jake the Runaway and Short Stories Told After Dark by "Uncle Remus,"* a bear disguised as a quality "gennelman" comes courting Callie Ann's mother, and Callie Ann must find a way to prevent her mom from marrying him. A cautionary note: Because the original folktales were written in the 1800s, Callie Ann's mother is portrayed in a manner today considered derogatory; this should be discussed with students beforehand. DH & DB

4.53   Schick, Eleanor. **Navajo Wedding Day: A Diné Marriage Ceremony.** Illustrated by Eleanor Schick. Marshall Cavendish, 1999. ISBN 0-7614-5031-9. Unpaged. Elementary–Intermediate. Fiction, Cross-cultural.

This Diné wedding story is told from the perspective of a young girl who is invited to the wedding but isn't Navajo. The wedding day preparations are being explained to the young guest, and the reader gets to see the rituals through her eyes. The blending of traditional ways with modern-day changes makes this a realistic peek into one aspect of Diné culture. The wedding ceremony and all its preparations were explained to the author by members of the Bitterwater clan in Shonto, Arizona. MBC

4.54   Shank, Ned. **The Sanyasin's First Day.** Illustrated by Catherine Stock. Marshall Cavendish, 1999. ISBN 0-7614-5055-6. Unpaged. Primary. Fiction.

This fictional tale of how the choices we make in life directly influence the lives of others is an excellent vehicle for examining the interdependence and connectedness of people. The illustrations depict the energy and diversity of life in India's major cities, but this is a story that could be retold anywhere. Although not recommended as a text for teaching students about life in India, the story is one that all readers will enjoy. (Visibility) LCJ

4.55   Smith, Cynthia L. **Jingle Dancer.** Illustrated by Cornelius Van Wright and Ying-Hwa Hu. Morrow, 2000. ISBN 0-688-16242-8. Unpaged. Primary–Intermediate. Fiction, Ethnic specific.

Jenna wants to dance at her first powwow, but she needs to collect more jingles for her dress. She learns that the generosity of family and friends can help solve her problem. This story shows Native American women in contemporary roles: lawyers and entrepreneurs as well as traditional dancers. It also reinforces the message that combining resources to help one another is better than depending on just one relationship. MBC

4.56   Staples, Suzanne Fisher. **Shiva's Fire.** Farrar, Straus and Giroux, 2000. ISBN 0-374-36824-4. 275 pp. Middle school. Fiction, World.

Parvati was born amidst the chaos of a cyclone that nearly destroyed her family's village in India. In the aftermath, it becomes clear that Parvati is different, and the villagers blame her for their misfortunes. Only the love of her mother, Meenakshi, shelters Parvati as her strange powers develop. When she is discovered by a famous guru, Parvati learns that dance is her dharma, her natural duty. And it is through dance that Parvati comes to understand that her differences are truly gifts. (Social Responsibility) TLC

4.57   Stock, Catherine. **Gugu's House.** Clarion, 2001. ISBN 0-618-00389-4. 32 pp. Primary. Fiction, World.

Young Kukamba, who lives in the city, is excited about visiting her grandmother, Gugu. Gugu is a storytelling artist who uses mud to make new walls and animal statues. She collects ashes from the night's fire for white paint and charcoal for black paint. Together Gugu and her granddaughter paint magnificent scenes on the walls and turn the mud statues into colorful, animated friends. When a burst of rain washes away the creations, Kukamba is heartbroken, but Gugu then teaches her about the cycle of nature. With the rains, new colors and creations can be found and molded. The endearing Gugu is based on a real Mrs. Khosa who lives in Zimbabwe near the Limpopo River. Her village is set in a desolate and dry area. Each year there's a rainstorm, and Mrs. Khosa always rebuilds her home with color and stories to be shared with all the neighborhood children. EMA

4.58   Strom, Maria Diaz. **Rainbow Joe and Me.** Illustrated by Maria Diaz Strom. Lee & Low, 1999. ISBN 1-880000-93-8. Unpaged. Primary. Fiction, Cross-cultural.

Eloise loves colors. Rainbow Joe loves jazz music. Eloise wonders how Rainbow Joe can mix colors since he's blind. Together Eloise and Rainbow Joe discover a new way to mix paints. The power of imagination and friendship come together to show Eloise that just because a person is blind doesn't mean he can't see. The bold colors and easy conversation between the two characters make this an easy and fun book to read. (Visibility) MBC

4.59   Stuve-Bodeen, Stephanie. **Mama Elizabeti.** Illustrated by Christy Hale. Lee & Low, 2000. ISBN 1-58430-002-7. Unpaged. Primary. Fiction, World.

Elizabeti no longer has to carry around a rock, pretending it's her baby. Now she has full responsibility for her little brother, Obedi, who doesn't lie quietly in one place! The story and illustrations in this sequel to *Elizabeti's Doll* are charming and captivating. NHK

4.60   Tan, Amy. **Sagwa, the Chinese Siamese Cat.** Illustrated by Gretchen Schields. Aladdin, 2001. ISBN 0-689-84617-7. Unpaged. Primary. Fiction, World.

Ming Maio tells her kittens the story of their ancestor Sagwa as a way of explaining the unusual markings that Siamese cats have had for centuries. This book is about the importance of acknowledging and being proud of one's ancestors. Although the story is about a Chinese cat in China, Chinese-style illustration is the only cultural element; the story itself is universal. Some readers, however, may find the stereotypical slanted eyes controversial, although the illustrations have been highly praised. IL

4.61   Taulbert, Clifton L. **Little Cliff's First Day of School.** Illustrated by E. B. Lewis. Dial, 2001. ISBN 0-8037-2557-4. Unpaged. Primary. Fiction, Ethnic specific.

This is another delightful story about Cliff and the Porch People. Cliff is having first-day-of-school jitters, and he keeps thinking up excuses for not having to go. Cliff's great-grandmother finally gets him to school, where he discovers that things won't be as difficult as he thought. MBC

4.62 Taylor, Mildred D. **The Land.** Phyllis Fogelman Books, 2001. ISBN 0-8037-1950-7. 375 pp. Middle School. Fiction, Ethnic specific.

The Land is the story of Paul-Edward Logan and his determination to acquire land in Mississippi during the 1880s. Paul-Edward is the son of a White plantation owner and a Black slave. While Paul-Edward had the privilege of growing up in his father's household and receiving an education, he is still denied access to and acceptance by the White world. Many readers will recall Paul-Edward as Cassie Logan's grandfather in the Newbery Medal–winning *Roll of Thunder, Hear My Cry*. Taylor continues to write about the strength of family ties and of humanity. (War and Resilience) EMA

4.63 Thomas, Joyce Carol. **A Mother's Heart, A Daughter's Love: Poems for Us to Share.** Joanna Cotler Books, 2001. ISBN 0-06-029649-6. 52 pp. Intermediate–Middle school. Fiction, Ethnic specific.

Joyce Carol Thomas has written numerous books and won numerous awards. This time she has used two voices to express the love between mother and daughter. In her collection of twenty-five poems, she captures the rhythms of life from a daughter's birth to a mother's death, including many of life's in-betweens, from toddler bath time fits to the first day of kindergarten. Thomas shares in her notes, "As in life, sometimes we stand alone, sometimes there's discord, and sometimes we are in perfect harmony." These poems are great for reading alone or with a parent. EMA

4.64 Tripp, Valerie. **Josefina's Song.** Illustrated by Jean-Paul Tribbles. Pleasant Company, 2001. ISBN 1-58485-272-0. 48 pp. Intermediate. Fiction.

Josefina's Song, part of The American Girls Collection series, takes place in the early 1800s. Ten-year-old Josefina accompanies her father into the New Mexico mountains to visit a shepherd camp to check on an elderly shepherd. When her father has an accident, Josefina brings him back to safety. Because Josefina and her family speak Spanish, some Spanish words are interspersed throughout the story. A Spanish glossary is provided as well as historical background on shepherd life during the 1800s. In addition, the author offers an explanation of how to weave a small rug. (Bilingual and Multilingual Literature) DH & DB

4.65   Velasquez, Eric. **Grandma's Records.** Walker, 2001. ISBN 0-8027-8760-6. Unpaged. Primary. Fiction, Ethnic specific.

During his summer visits to El Barrio, Eric's grandma introduces him to the pleasures of music. Eric's appreciation of *bomba y plena*, salsa, and merengue hits a high note when his grandma gets them backstage passes to a New York City club. Through music, Eric builds a loving relationship with his grandmother. The muted oil painting illustrations impart a sense of time and place, and the short biographies of Puerto Rican musicians at the back of the book provide helpful context. (Bilingual and Multilingual Literature) TLC

4.66   Vizurraga, Susan. **Miss Opal's Auction.** Illustrated by Mark Graham. Henry Holt, 2000. ISBN 0-8050-5891-5. Unpaged. Primary–Adult. Fiction.

In this beautiful story of an elderly African American woman and her neighbor, a young European American girl, a precious friendship is shared. But when Miss Opal decides to sell her home and everything in it to live in a retirement home, the young girl becomes sad. This is a touching story of an interracial, intergenerational friendship between two special individuals. MVW

4.67   Wahl, Jan. **Rosa's Parrot.** Illustrated by Kim Howard. Whispering Coyote, 1999. ISBN 1-58-089-011-3. Unpaged. Primary. Fiction, Cross-cultural.

What will Rosa do with her parrot, Pico? Mischievous Pico helps Rosa, who is hard of hearing, by repeating conversations loudly for her—except when he gets into one of his naughty moods. This delightful, heartwarming story with vibrant illustrations will bring enjoyment to children of all ages. DH & DB

4.68 Watson, Kim. **Just Like Dad.** Illustrated by Daniel M. Kanemoto. Simon Spotlight, 2001. ISBN 0-689-83999-5. Unpaged. Primary. Fiction, Ethnic specific.

Just Like Dad is based on the TV series *Little Bill* created by Bill Cosby and is one in the Little Bill series that "encourages children to value their family and friends, to feel good about themselves, and to learn to solve problems creatively." In this story, Little Bill shares the day with Big Bill at his workplace. Dad helps Little Bill see the parallels of going to work and going to school. Young readers will delight in making comparisons to their own parents' workplaces. The simple dialogue and narrative make this an excellent book for early readers. EMA

4.69 Winter, Jeanette. **My Baby.** Illustrated by Jeanette Winter. Frances Foster Books, 2001. ISBN 0-374-35103-1. Unpaged. Primary. Fiction, World.

A first-time mother tells about learning to paint cloth and how this knowledge serves her Mali village. It also occupies her time as she awaits her baby's birth. When the baby is born, the loving mother welcomes "my baby" by wrapping it in the cloth she painted. The bold illustrations highlight the beauty of the textile painting. NHK

4.70 Wong, Janet S. **Behind the Wheel: Poems about Driving.** Margaret K. McElderry Books, 1999. ISBN 0-689-82531-5. 44 pp. Middle school and up. Fiction, Ethnic specific.

"Forget kindergarten, sharing. Everything you need to know you learn right here behind the wheel." In this collection of poems about driving and the experience of cars, Janet Wong looks at driving as a metaphor for life. This distinctively American theme is retold through Asian American eyes. (Visibility) MBC

4.71 Wong, Janet S. **Night Garden: Poems from the World of Dreams.** Illustrated by Julie Paschkis. Margaret K. McElderry Books, 2000. ISBN 0-689-82617-6. 30 pp. Primary and up. Fiction, Ethnic specific.

This is another eclectic collection by the widely known poet and author Janet Wong. The night garden is a place for dreaming: "Deep in the earth a tangle of roots sends up green shoots and dreams grow wild." Wong's poems range from the gentle and bemusing to the dark and scary. This collection contains a great range of poems for exploring the power of dreams. MBC

4.72   Wong, Janet S. **The Rainbow Hand: Poems about Mothers and Children.** Illustrated by Jennifer Hewitson. Margaret K. McElderry Books, 1999. ISBN 0-689-82148-4. 26 pp. Middle school and up. Fiction, Ethnic specific.

In this collection of poems, Janet Wong tells stories about the experiences of being mothered and of being a mother. She explores many different aspects of motherhood, along with a child's perspective of her mother. Inspired by memories of her own mother and the joy of being a mother herself, Wong delivers a wonderful tribute to mothers everywhere. MBC

4.73   Wong, Janet S. **The Trip Back Home.** Illustrated by Bo Jia. Harcourt, 2000. ISBN 0-15-200784-9. 32 pp. Primary. Fiction, Ethnic specific.

Author Janet Wong recounts a childhood trip she took with her mother to visit her Korean grandparents and family. Delicately illustrated by Bo Jia, the story interweaves the recollections of a simple gift exchange with the importance of bridging family ties across the generations, cultures, and language differences. EMA

4.74   Woodson, Jacqueline. **Miracle's Boys.** Putnam's, 2000. ISBN 0-399-23113-7. 133 pp. Intermediate–Middle school. Fiction, Ethnic specific.

This painfully powerful novel tells the story of three orphaned brothers who struggle to overcome tragedy, poverty, grief, and gang violence. The streetwise brothers live in New York City and are under the care of their eldest brother, Ty'ree. Each brother must deal with his own emotional baggage and set of demons. To survive, the boys hang on to the dying promise of their mother, Miracle, that "she's too deep inside of us" to ever completely leave them. Eventually the boys learn to rely on one another through their love, "brother to brother to brother." Once again Woodson reveals how emotional struggle can be transformed into hope. EMA

Coretta Scott King Award, 2001; Los Angeles Times Book Prize, 2001

4.75   Woodson, Jacqueline. **The Other Side.** Illustrated by Earl B. Lewis. Putnam's, 2001. ISBN 0-399-23116-1. Unpaged. Primary. Fiction, Ethnic specific.

In a simple prose style, Jacqueline Woodson tells this story of friendship across a fence that divides Blacks from Whites. Clover, a young African American girl, lives on one side of the fence. Annie, a European American child, lives on the other. Both are instructed not to climb over the fence. As the summer progresses, however, the girls introduce themselves and convince each other, as well as their friends, that "a fence like this was made for sitting on." By the end of the season, the fence no longer separates, and the two make a pact that "someday somebody's going to come along and knock this old fence down." Lewis's delicate watercolor illustrations blend beautifully with this story of hope, honesty, and innocence. (Visibility) EMA

4.76   Yep, Laurence. **The Amah.** Putnam's, 1999. ISBN 0-399-23040-8. 181 pp. Ages Intermediate–Middle school. Fiction.

With the death of her father and her mother's new job as an "amah" or governess to twelve-year-old Stephanie, Amy Chin must now take on more responsibility for the house and her four younger siblings. She will also miss her rehearsals for her role as a stepsister in her ballet school's performance of *Cinderella*. While learning to make accommodations in her family life, Amy gradually gains insight into her stepsister role. Gradually Amy and Stephanie reach out to each other, bridging the tension between them, as they realize the bond they share. Interwoven into the issues of friendship and family ties is the struggle and resolution Amy must find with the generations of her immigrant family. EMA

4.77   Yep, Laurence. **Angelfish.** Putnam's, 2001. ISBN 0-399-23041-6. 217 pp. Middle School. Fiction, Ethnic specific.

In this sequel to *The Cook's Family*, Robin, an aspiring ballerina, finds herself working in Mr. Tsow's fish store to pay for the window she accidentally broke. It turns out that Mr. Tsow is a former ballet dancer from China and a victim of the Chinese Cultural Revolution. Mr. Tsow resents Robin's biracial heritage and often disparages her for it. Robin is confused because she feels part Chinese and part American but not fully a part of either world. In the end, Robin's love of ballet and dedication to the shop overcome Mr. Tsow's distrust of a "half-person." MBC

4.78   Yin. **Coolies.** Illustrated by Chris K. Soentpiet. Philomel, 2001. ISBN 0-399-23227-3. Unpaged. All ages. Fiction, Ethnic specific.

The book's title, *Coolies,* is a demeaning term to Chinese Americans. But Yin, a Chinese American raised in Manhattan, decided to challenge political correctness by using the term to praise and acknowledge the immigrant Chinese railroad builders of nineteenth-century United States. Yin tells her story through Paw-Paw, grandmother, who prepares a feast to honor *bokgong,* great-grandfather Shek, and his brother Little Wong, both of whom leave Canton for California in the mid-1800s. Their journey in the United States includes encounters with racism and prejudice, harsh weather and avalanches, and dangerous work conditions. They survive the four long years and accomplish the incredible feat of helping to build the first transcontinental railroad. Artist Chris Soentpiet brings incredible life to this historical novel by highlighting emotional features and recreating breathtaking landscapes. EMA

A.

B.

C.

D.

A. *La procesión de Naty [Naty's Parade]*, Gina Freschet (**1.9**).   **B.** *Bud, Not Buddy*, Christopher Paul Curtis (**2.10**).   **C.** *One True Friend*, Joyce Hansen (**2.18**).   **D.** *It Doesn't Have to Be This Way: A Barrio Story/No tiene que ser así: Una historia del barrio*, Luis J. Rodríguez/Daniel Galvez (**1.16**).

A.

B.

C.

D.

A. *Ida B. Wells: Mother of the Civil Rights Movement,* Dennis Brindell Fradin and Judith Bloom Fradin (**2.15**). **B.** *Flowers from Mariko,* Rick Noguchi and Deneen Jenks/Michelle Reiko Kumata (**2.28**). **C.** *A Special Fate: Chiune Sugihara, Hero of the Holocaust,* Alison Leslie Gold (**3.11**). **D.** *One Boy from Kosovo,* Trish Marx/Cindy Karp (**2.23**).

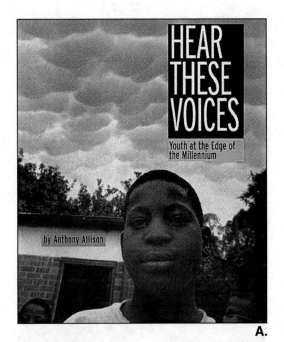

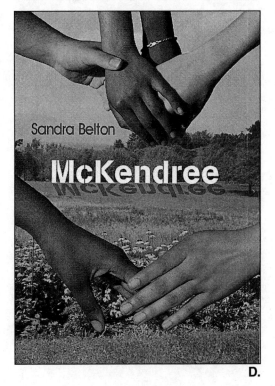

A. *Hear These Voices: Youth at the Edge of the Millennium,* Anthony Allison (**3.2**).   **B.** *If a Bus Could Talk: The Story of Rosa Parks,* Faith Ringgold (**3.26**).   **C.** *Esperanza Rising,* Pam Muñoz Ryan (**3.29**). **D.** *McKendree,* Sandra Belton (**3.4**).

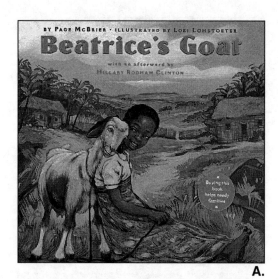

A.

B.

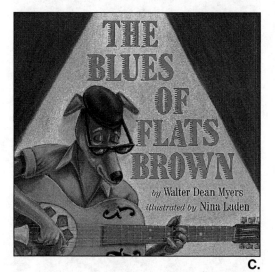

C.

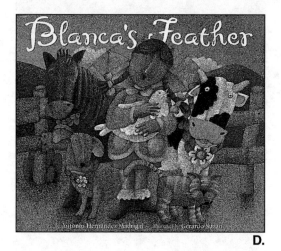

D.

A. *Beatrice's Goat,* Page McBrier/Lori Lohstoeter (**3.18**). **B.** *Barbara Jordan: Getting Things Done,* James Mendelsohn (**3.19**). **C.** *The Blues of Flats Brown,* Walter Dean Myers/Nina Laden (**4.37**). **D.** *Blanca's Feather,* Antonio Hernández Madrigal/Gerardo Suzán (**4.33**).

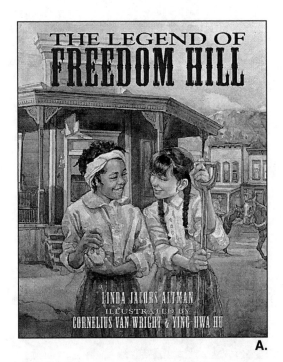

A.

B.

C.

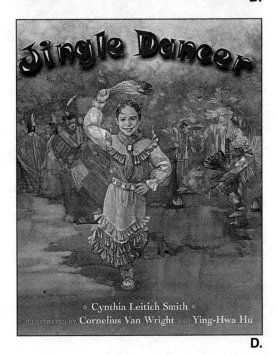

D.

A. *The Legend of Freedom Hill*, Linda Jacobs Altman/Cornelius Van Wright and Ying-Hwa Hu (**4.2**).
B. *Weave Little Stars into My Sleep: Native American Lullabies*, Neil Philip/Edward S. Curtis (**4.45**).
C. *A Single Shard*, Linda Sue Park (**4.43**).　　**D.** *Jingle Dancer*, Cynthia L. Smith/Cornelius Van Wright and Ying-Hwa Hu (**4.55**).

A.

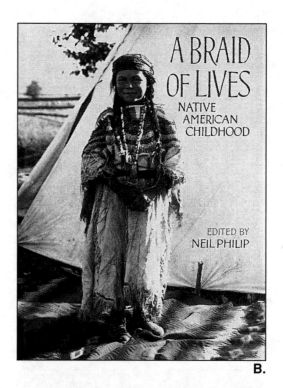

B.

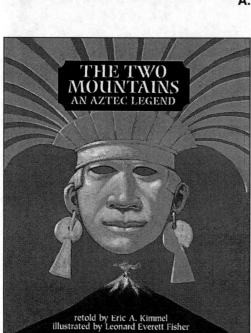

C.

D.

A. *Coolies,* Yin/Chris K. Soentpiet (**4.78**).   **B.** *A Braid of Lives: Native American Childhood,* Neil Philip (**5.37**).   **C.** *The Two Mountains: An Aztec Legend,* Eric A. Kimmel/Leonard Everett Fisher (**5.23**). **D.** *Hurry Freedom: African Americans in Gold Rush California,* Jerry Stanley (**5.42**).

A.

B.

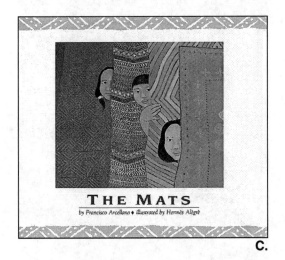

C.

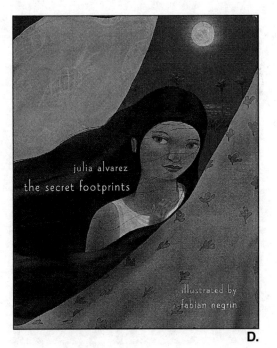

D.

A. *Tallchief: America's Prima Ballerina,* Maria Tallchief with Rosemary Wells/Gary Kelley (**5.45**). **B.** *Kids Dance: The Students of Ballet Tech,* Jim Varriale (**5.46**). **C.** *The Mats,* Francisco Arcellana/Hermès Alègrè (**6.3**). **D.** *The Secret Footprints,* Julia Alvarez/Fabian Negrin (**6.2**).

A.

B.

C.

D.

A. *Grannie and the Jumbie: A Caribbean Tale,* Margaret M. Hurst (**6.14**).　**B.** *This Next New Year,* Janet S. Wong/Yangsook Choi (**6.28**).　**C.** *Can You Top That?,* W. Nikola-Lisa/Hector Viveros Lee (**6.18**). **D.** *Words with Wings: A Treasury of African-American Poetry and Art,* Belinda Rochelle (**6.21**).

5 Informative and Educational Books

Donald T. Mizokawa

Artificial ignorance* has persisted far too long, but AI is curable within our lifetimes. Because of the tradition in American literature of compelling works that instruct and inform, this volume of *Kaleidoscope* includes a section on works that teach, especially about subjects about which misconceptions and stereotypes are commonplace. *Africa Is Not a Country* (Knight & Melnicove, 2000), for example, is a work that counters the widespread and erroneous use of the name *Africa* to denote a unitary political entity rather than a continent that enfolds a virtually infinite collection of peoples, histories, cultures, languages, mores, religious beliefs, and ethnicities.

Ignorance is not inevitable, despite its existence at all levels of society. During the Watergate hearings into the "dirty tricks" planned and executed by President Richard Nixon's supporters, one attorney for Nixon referred to Senator Daniel Inouye of Hawaii as a "little Jap." When confronted by the media about the offensive words, the attorney said, "He could call me 'a little American.'" The attorney missed more than one point. First, the term *Jap* is generally perceived as an offensive epithet, not a shorthand term. Second, Inouye is no more Japanese than Richard Nixon. Both are native-born Americans. How could an educated person—a lawyer at the national level—not know?

At an awards banquet for distinguished student scholars of color, the president of one major western university joked about whether a Spanish-surnamed student had a green card. Following the media and community uproar, the president apologized and volunteered for cultural sensitivity training. How could he not know?

Research into social distance describes the immense personal and communal benefits of familiarity and knowledge. Physically able people who encounter and interact with people in wheelchairs, for instance,

---

*This particular use of the term *AI* is attributed to Click and Clack, the Tappet Brothers, "Car Talk₍®₎," broadcast date June 30, 2001, National Public Radio, on the day after the premiere of the theater movie *AI*.

begin to lose their fear and distrust of people with different abilities. Despite the powerfully negative implications of the common disclaimer, "Why, one of my best friends is [fill in the blank]," intimate social distance does engender tolerance, then acceptance. Literature can help narrow the social distance by fostering a reader's intimate knowledge of what otherwise is unknown and unfamiliar, to the point even of xenophobia. The exotic becomes quotidian.

We had hoped that the works in this section would enable us to suspend the publication of *Kaleidoscope* in a world in which the Western literary canon fully encompasses the great literature of *all* American peoples and in which the Great Books of the Western world for children include entries that were first profiled here. But our hope for the dearth, if not the death, of AI seems premature.

5.1   Adler, David A. **A Picture Book of George Washington Carver.** Illustrated by Dan Brown. Holiday House, 1999. ISBN 0-8234-1429-9. Unpaged. Primary. Biography.

For teachers looking for biographies of African Americans, this book is historically accurate and well written. The author includes many direct quotes from George Washington Carver, which gives readers a sense of learning from Carver as well as learning about him. (War and Resilience) LCJ

5.2   Ajmera, Maya, and John D. Ivanko. **Back to School.** Charlesbridge, 2001. ISBN 1-57091-383-8. Unpaged. Primary and up. Nonfiction, World.

This delightful book from the authors of *To Be a Kid* depicts the "trials and triumphs of school life in thirty-seven countries around the world." An amazing collection of photos, along with inviting and educational text, shows the reader that school is a place to learn, no matter where the school is located. The book dispels stereotypes and the notion that emerging nations are "backwards, or uneducated." This is a must for every elementary classroom. (Families, Friends, and Community) MBC

5.3   Ajmera, Maya, and John D. Ivanko. **To Be a Kid.** Charlesbridge, 1999. ISBN 0-881-06-842-X. Unpaged. Primary–Intermediate. Nonfiction, World.

Through brilliant photographs of children and their families around the world, Ajmera and Ivanko convey the idea that children from diverse cultures share a love of play and love for family and friends. This book illustrates what it means "to be a kid," regardless of heritage. (Families, Friends, and Community) DH & DB

5.4 Batten, Mary. **Anthropologist: Scientist of the People.** Photographs by A. Magdalena Hurtado and Kim Hill. Houghton Mifflin, 2001. ISBN 0-618-08368-5. 64 pp. Intermediate–Middle school. Nonfiction.

Batten's text introduces young people to anthropology through Magdalena Hurtado, a human evolutionary ecologist who studies the few remaining hunter-gatherer cultures. Readers learn about the questions, tools, and methods of anthropologists. The book focuses on the work that Hurtado and her husband, Kim Hill, have done with the Ache people of Paraguay. Pictures and descriptions provide information about the everyday life of the Ache and connect that life to our past as human beings. Hurtado raises questions about the future of the Ache people. (Social Responsibility) TLC

5.5 Borden, Louise, and Mary Kay Kroeger. **Fly High! The Story of Bessie Coleman.** Illustrated by Teresa Flavin. Margaret K. McElderry Books, 2001. ISBN 0-689-82456-2. Unpaged. Primary. Biography.

This book, with its simple prose and quiet, warm illustrations, brings a powerful message to children. Bessie Coleman overcame many obstacles in her quest to someday be *somebody*. Eventually Bessie became the first African American woman to earn a pilot's license. But Bessie didn't stop there. It was important to her that, wherever she went, she spread her message to African American children. In her own words, "You can be *somebody*. You can fly high, just like me." (Social Responsibility; War and Resilience) TLC

5.6 Bradshaw, Douglas. **Shaquille O'Neal: Man of Steel.** Grosset & Dunlap, 2001. ISBN 0-448-42552-1. 48 pp. Primary–Middle school. Biography.

The All Aboard Reading series includes a collection of both nonfiction and fiction, mainly the former. The stories of sports heroes are popular in collections such as this. Certainly, stories about O'Neal are of high interest to young readers, and this version of his life will capture the interest of sports buffs. The text does contain some minor errors that a vigilant editor would have caught and revised. (Visibility; Families, Friends, and Community) NHK

5.7   Chen, Kerstin, reteller. **Lord of the Cranes: A Chinese Tale.** Illustrated by Jian Jiang Chen. Translated by J. Alison James. North-South, 2000. ISBN 0-7358-1192-X. Unpaged. Primary–Intermediate. Fiction, World.

Although the independent reading level of this book is third grade, this is a story that should be included at any grade level if the class is studying Chinese history or Chinese culture. The author states that she has translated this classic Chinese story into English so that a wider audience can learn from the model life of the Lord of the Cranes, a wise man who disguises himself in order to go out into the world to find people who are kind and generous. The vibrant illustrations match the rich narration of this Chinese tale of kindness, community, and beauty. (Families, Friends, and Community) LCJ

5.8   Clark, Domini. **South Africa, the Land.** Crabtree, 2000. ISBN 0-86505-315-4. 32 pp. Intermediate–Middle school. Nonfiction, World.

This book provides an overview of the varied characteristics of South Africa. Part of The Lands, Peoples, and Cultures series, this book would be an excellent supplementary reading text for any middle school language arts or social studies teacher who is pulling together materials for a unit on South Africa. The book comprises two- to five-page chapters that are easily accessible for intermediate readers. LCJ

5.9   Cooper, Michael L. **Fighting for Honor: Japanese Americans and World War II.** Clarion, 2000. ISBN 0-395-91375-6. 118 pp. Intermediate–Middle school. Nonfiction, Cross-cultural.

Through first-person testimony, Cooper vividly chronicles the lives of Japanese Americans during World War II, grabbing the attention of young historians by setting the scene of Pearl Harbor and describing prejudice against Japanese Americans and the formation of the internment camps. Throughout his tale, he highlights the contradictions and ironies inherent in the policies set by President Roosevelt and the U.S. government. Cooper trumpets the honorable contributions of those Japanese Americans serving in the Military Intelligence Service and the 100th and 442nd battalions, "the most highly decorated unit in the U.S. military history." The final chapter, "Returning Home," details the stamina needed for survival and ends with a reminder that "the U.S., through its Constitution and laws, promises equal and fair treatment to all of its people. It had betrayed that promise, and this betrayal can never be completely forgotten by the betrayed." Photos, maps, chronologies, and references supplement this historical text. (War and Resilience) EMA

5.10   Demi. **Gandhi.** Margaret K. McElderry Books, 2001. ISBN 0-689-84149-3. Unpaged. All ages. Biography, World.

Once again Demi presents the biography of a historical figure with as much brilliance and detail as her illustrative paintings. She begins with Mohandas Karamchand Gandhi as a small, shy boy who barely graduates from high school, and then simply yet substantively highlights Gandhi's life transformation from a law student, to an "English gentleman" practicing law in South Africa, to his return to India, where he lived a simpler, self-reliant life and employed the nonviolent tactics that continue to influence people throughout the world. This book captures the spirit and essence of this extraordinary man. (Social Responsibility) EMA

5.11   Ercelawn, Ayesha. **New Zealand.** Gareth Stevens, 2001. ISBN 0-8368-2332-X. 96 pp. Elementary–Middle school. Nonfiction, World.

The author provides a broad view of New Zealand: its history, societies, cultures, and geography. The photographs are plentiful and interesting and add strength and vibrancy to the text. The editor notes that this Countries of the World series provides a "country's past and present relations with the United States and Canada which does ground it in contemporary life for the young reader." The end of each book lists Web sites (with a listing of key words to aid in finding new sites), videotapes, and books that readers can investigate. Teachers should note that the traumatic impact of colonization on indigenous peoples is treated in a cursory manner. (Visibility) NHK

5.12   Farley, Carol. **The King's Secret: The Legend of King Sejong.** Illustrated by Robert Jew. HarperCollins, 2001. ISBN 0-688-12776-2. Unpaged. Primary. Fiction, World.

As the author mentions in an author's note, although the story is fiction, it is based on Korea's King Sejong, who invented the Korean alphabetical system. Chong In-ji, a character in the story, is also a historical figure. A helpful note about the Korean language system is provided. Although the illustrator tried to catch authentic features of Koreans and their culture, his illustrations of a Korean boy with a big head and slanted eyes might be considered offensive by some. IL

5.13   George-Warren, Holly. **Shake, Rattle & Roll: The Founders of Rock & Roll.** Illustrated by Laura Levine. Houghton Mifflin, 2001. ISBN 0-618-05540-1. Unpaged. Intermediate–Middle school. Biography, Cross-cultural.

Little Richard, Elvis Presley, LaVern Baker, Carl Perkins, Richie Valens—these are just some of the famous rockers whose influences helped make rock 'n' roll a musical and cultural phenomenon. This book is a light introduction to some of the people who influenced this American music style. The portraits of each artist are illustrated in a kitschy, folk-art style, and the prose is spirited (if a little corny and cleaned up). Kids might enjoy using this as a model for putting together their own hall-of-fame-style history. TLC

5.14   Goble, Paul. **Storm Maker's Tipi.** Illustrated by Paul Goble. Atheneum, 2001. ISBN 0-689-84137-X. Unpaged. Primary–Intermediate. Myth/folklore, Cross-cultural.

The Great Spirit's helper, Napi, gave First Man and First Woman shelter by teaching them how to make a tipi. This story, accompanied by detailed drawings and directions, is followed by a related tale, about how Storm Maker saved Sacred Otter, a leader of the Blackfeet people, and his son and showed him protective designs to paint on his tipi. The book includes a photograph of tipis pitched in a modern Blackfeet summer camp, as well as a reproducible outline for making a paper tipi. TLC

5.15   Hazen-Hammond, Susan. **Thunder Bear and Ko: The Buffalo Nation and Nambe Pueblo.** Photographs by Susan Hazen-Hammond. Dutton, 1999. ISBN 0-525-46013-6. Unpaged. Intermediate. Nonfiction.

Eight-year-old Thunder Bear tells about the care and keeping of buffalo (*ko* in the Tewa language). With the reestablishment of the buffalo, people at Nambe Pueblo began to reconnect with traditions and beliefs of the past. The book shows a fascinating blend of traditional rituals unique to Nambe Pueblo and other, nontraditional activities. This vital combination of old and new leaves the reader feeling that Tewa culture is thriving and well, not just a part of history. (Social Responsibility; Friends, Families, and Community) MBC

5.16   Hill, Anne E. **Denzel Washington.** Chelsea House, 2000. ISBN 0-7910-4692-3. 92 pp. Middle school. Biography.

For middle school teachers looking for excellent examples of biographies of African Americans, this is a book that should be in their collection. The work provides an accurate, detailed history of the life of Academy Award–winning actor Denzel Washington. It also gives readers insight into the struggles that African American actors still have to face at times in contemporary United States. Washington's voice is heard throughout the book and, as a result, his strength, wisdom, and talent come alive. LCJ

5.17   Holdsclaw, Chamique, with Jennifer Frey. **Chamique Holdsclaw: My Story.** Aladdin, 2001. ISBN 0-689-83592-2. 176 pp. Intermediate–Middle school. Autobiography, Ethnic specific.

When Chamique Holdsclaw tells the story of her rise to basketball stardom, she tells it straight, discussing the struggles she faced growing up in Astoria, Queens. But Chamique is proud of the hard work she put in both on and off the court, and she's proud of where she came from. Chamique weaves together the stories of her growth as a basketball player and reflections on the values and ideals she learned from the grandmother who raised her. (Families, Friends, and Community) TLC

5.18   Hoyt-Goldsmith, Diane. **Las Posadas: An Hispanic Christmas Celebration.** Photographs by Lawrence Migdale. Holiday

House, 1999. ISBN 0-8234-1449-3. 32 pp. Intermediate. Nonfiction, Cross-cultural.

Through the perspective of eleven-year-old Kristen Lucero and her community in New Mexico, Hoyt-Goldsmith explores the celebration of the nine nights of Las Posadas. This is an excellent informational book about Las Posadas, including the history, songs, and recipes of this holiday. A glossary of Spanish words relating to this celebration is included. The photographs by Lawrence Migdale bring Las Posadas to life. (Visibility) DH & DB

5.19   Kalman, Bobbie. **Life in a Longhouse Village.** Crabtree, 2001. ISBN 0-7787-0370-3. 32 pp. Intermediate. Nonfiction, Cross-cultural.

One in Bobbie Kalman's Native Nations of North America series, this book is about the Iroquois, Native Americans who shared a common way of life, living in longhouses. Some of the information overlaps with Kalman's other books, such as *Native Homes* and *Nations of the Plains*. Readers will be impressed that the Iroquois's efforts to protect their environment started much earlier than anybody else's. (Families, Friends, and Community) IL

5.20   Kalman, Bobbie. **Native Homes.** Crabtree, 2001. ISBN 0-7787-0371-1. 32 pp. Primary–Intermediate. Nonfiction, Cross-cultural.

This book is packed with information about the houses/homes of Native Americans in North America. Every reader will find information on Native American homes of their own region because houses are described according to weather and, consequently, region. Wonderfully detailed illustrations help children understand the text. Explanations of physical aspects of houses are naturally interwoven with descriptions of Native American lifestyles and ways of coping with nature. Above all, the tribes are depicted as collaborative, innovative, and smart. A glossary and index are provided. IL

5.21   Kimmel, Eric A. **The Jar of Fools: Eight Hanukkah Stories from Chelm.** Illustrated by Mordicai Gerstein. Holiday House, 2000. ISBN 0-8234-1463-9. 56 pp. Primary–Intermediate. Fiction, World.

At the end of this collection, the author reveals that "the real city of Chelm is located in eastern Poland, approximately forty kilometers from the border of Ukraine. However, the Chelm of Jewish legend can be anywhere in Eastern Europe." This collection of stories masterfully illustrates the wisdom, values, humor, and character of Jewish culture. Readers will not only learn about Jewish culture, but also have the opportunity to reflect on the nature of the human spirit. (War and Resilience) LCJ

5.22   Kimmel, Eric A. **Montezuma and the Fall of the Aztecs.** Illustrated by Daniel San Souci. Holiday House, 2000. ISBN 0-8234-1452-3. Unpaged. Intermediate. Historical nonfiction.

Teachers looking for a historical reference book that provides factual information about the Aztecs and the conquest of the Spanish explorer Cortez will find this book an excellent resource. Recreating this era through narrative, Kimmel provides an engaging account of the rise and fall of Montezuma and the Aztec civilization. The author also includes a glossary and a reference section at the end of the book in order to supplement the reader's understanding. LCJ

5.23   Kimmel, Eric A. **The Two Mountains: An Aztec Legend.** Illustrated by Leonard Everett Fisher. Holiday House, 2000. ISBN 0-8234-1504-X. Unpaged. Primary–Middle school. Myth/folklore, World.

This Aztec legend, as retold by Eric Kimmel, recounts the story of two young lovers who disobey the elders wishes in order to fulfill their own desires. Like the story of Romeo and Juliet, the couple's choices lead to dire consequences. Teachers interested in the history of Mexico as well as cultural stories will find this a useful resource for any classroom. (Families, Friends, and Community) LCJ

5.24   Knight, Margy Burns, and Mark Melnicove. **Africa Is Not a Country.** Illustrated by Anne Sibley O'Brien. Millbrook, 2000. ISBN 0-7613-1266-8. 39 pp. Primary–Intermediate. Nonfiction, World.

Through the stories of a child's day in all parts of Africa, this book captures the vitality and diversity that make up the African continent. The authors expertly weave in factual information with narration, and the illustrations accurately depict the people and the situations described in the stories. A glossary gives some basic descriptions of the countries represented. This book is highly recommended for grades 3 through 6. LCJ

5.25   Krohn, Katherine. **Ella Fitzgerald: First Lady of Song.** Lerner, 2001. ISBN 0-8225-4933-6. 112 pp. Middle school–Intermediate. Biography, Cross-cultural.

Ella Fitzgerald was a powerful figure in American music. This biography spans her career from her days on the streets of Harlem at age seventeen to her receiving the National Medal of Arts. Because Fitzgerald was so much a part of the scene and continued to grow as an artist, her story is also the story of jazz. Fitzgerald's talent stretched from swing to bebop to her famous songbooks of American composers. The book includes photos, a time line, and resources for further exploration. TLC

5.26   Markel, Rita J. **Jimi Hendrix.** Lerner, 2001. ISBN 0-8225-9697-0. 112 pp. Intermediate–Middle school. Biography.

This biography chronicles Jimi Hendrix's rocky climb to musical stardom. From early on, music provided a way for the shy boy to express himself, and it was his gift for doing so through the guitar that brought him fame. But allowing music to be his voice sometimes left his listeners confused and Hendrix frustrated to be heard as something more than a stage spectacle. His tragic death came just when Hendrix seemed to be pulling together both his private life and his career. This book is one in the A&E Biography series. (Social Responsibility) TLC

5.27   Marrin, Albert. **Tatan'ka Iyota'ke: Sitting Bull and His World.** Dutton, 2000. ISBN 0-525-45944-8. 246 pp. Intermediate–Middle school. Biography.

This is a well-documented biographical narrative of one of America's most noteworthy and heroic leaders. While we learn about Sitting Bull's unique ability to understand and bridge the Native American and European American worlds, we also gain insight into customs of Sitting Bull's people. Marrin pulls the reader into the story's time and setting to detail the Hunkpapa Lakota tribe's daily lives, rituals of the buffalo, and finally the murder of Sitting Bull and the Battle of

Wounded Knee. (War and Resilience; Families, Friends, and Community) EMA

5.28 Martin, Jacqueline Briggs. **The Lamp, the Ice, and the Boat Called** *Fish*. Illustrated by Beth Krommes. Houghton Mifflin, 2001. ISBN 0-618-00341-X. Unpaged. Intermediate. Fiction, Cross-cultural.

In 1913 an icy, winter shipwreck trapped a scientific expedition in the Canadian Arctic for more than a year. Without the help of the Inupiat family that accompanied them, the entire group would surely have perished in the unforgiving environment. The incredible scratchboard artwork and details of Inupiat culture bring this true story to life in a way that sets readers on the edge of their seats awaiting rescue. This book can serve as a powerful enticement for getting young people interested in history. (War and Resilience) TLC

5.29 McCollum, Sean. **Kenya.** Carolrhoda, 1999. ISBN 1-57505-105-2. 47 pp. Intermediate. Nonfiction, World.

The Globe Trotters Club series, to which *Kenya* belongs, is a bit more advanced than the A Ticket to . . . series by the same publisher. The style is breezy and engaging, while the text provides enough general information that readers will see the larger picture of the people and environment of Kenya. This is a well-organized and excellent social studies resource for teachers and students. (Families, Friends, and Community) NHK

5.30 McKissack, Fredrick Jr. **Black Hoops: The History of African-Americans in Basketball.** Scholastic, 1999. ISBN 0-590-48712-4. 154 pp. Intermediate–Middle school. Nonfiction, Ethnic specific.

McKissack has written a book that will appeal particularly to both men's basketball experts and novices, but aficionados of women's basketball should also find much to interest them. Beginning in 1891 with James Naismith's invention of a game that involved a soccer ball and two peach baskets and that was used to challenge and focus a rowdy class of YMCA students, this story details the rise of men's basketball to national passion. The book highlights the integral role that African American athletes had in making basketball a national sport. The final chapter is dedicated to the accomplishments of women in basketball as well as of African American athletes in the WNBA and the women's Olympic "dream team." LCJ

5.31 Mesenas, Geraldine, and Frederick Fisher. **Welcome to Israel.** Gareth Stevens, 2001. ISBN 0-8368-2519-5. 48 pp. Intermediate. Nonfiction, World.

This series is written in an interesting, engaging voice that will encourage reluctant readers of nonfiction to give it a try. Readers learn about the past and present geography, history, and culture of Israel. Political issues are addressed but not in any depth—not a disadvantage for young readers, who often benefit from beginning with a general overview of a country. The plentiful use of photographs portraying children of Israel helps young readers connect with other children and their lives in a distant land. As with the series for older children, each text in the Welcome to My Country series provides lists of related Web sites (with key words for additional searches), videotapes, and books. The series makes a useful collection in any classroom. (War and Resilience; Families, Friends, and Community) NHK

5.32 Monceaux, Morgan, and Ruth Katcher. **My Heroes, My People: African Americans and Native Americans in the West.** Illustrated by Morgan Monceaux. Frances Foster Books, 1999. ISBN 0-374-30770-9. 63 pp. Elementary–Adult. Nonfiction.

This remarkable collection of biographies of African American and Native American heroes of the American West comes to life through lively prose and vivid illustrations. Historical notes, legends, and previously untold stories about the struggles of famous and infamous historical figures to be free Americans are eloquently recounted in short excerpts. The authors also examine the historical roots of racially mixed people in the United States. Chapter subheadings range from Cowboys and Women to Buffalo Soldiers and Black and Red United. Young readers and adults alike will find this picture book of historical accounts an excellent resource. MVW

5.33 Morgan, Terri. **Ruthie Bolton-Holifield: Sharpshooting Playmaker.** Lerner, 1999. ISBN 0-8225-3666-8. 64 pp. Intermediate–Middle school. Biography.

This is a brief, easy-to-read biography that tells the story of Ruthie Bolton-Holifield's career from shooting hoops in the field next door to her hard-won Olympic gold medal. But Sacramento Monarchs player Bolton-Holifield is more than just a basketball player. In college she also earned academic honors while taking part in the campus ROTC. She's a devoted wife and a member of a large, musical family. Recently they made an album together. The book includes statistics, an index, and a glossary. (Families, Friends, and Community) TLC

5.34   Myers, Walter Dean. **At Her Majesty's Request: An African Princess in Victorian England.** Scholastic, 1999. ISBN 0-590-48669-1. 146 pp. Middle school. Biography, World.

Walter Dean Myers has done it again. He's found an important story to be told and taken great pains to be both accurate and engaging in the telling. In this work, Myers recounts the life of Sarah Forbes Bonetta, an Egbadan princess who became a close acquaintance of Queen Victoria of England. This book is an excellent choice for American or world history classes, as well as for the language arts curriculum in general. (War and Resilience) LCJ

5.35   Oluonye, Mary N. **South Africa.** Carolrhoda, 1999. ISBN 1-57505-141-9. 48 pp. Primary. Nonfiction, World.

Teachers often have difficulty finding social studies resources that primary grade children find informative, readable, and interesting. In its series A Ticket to . . . [a wide variety of countries and geographical locations from South African to Mexico], Carolrhoda Books enhances its excellent reputation for quality nonfiction children's texts. The illustrations and text are equally engaging and provide just enough information to give students a general overview of the politics, people, languages, and cultures of South Africa. (Families, Friends, and Community) NHK

5.36   Orgill, Roxane. **Shout, Sister, Shout! Ten Girl Singers Who Shaped a Century.** Margaret K. McElderry Books, 2001. ISBN 0-689-81991-9. 148 pp. Middle school. Biography.

To appeal to young readers who may never have heard of some of the incredible female singers of different decades and in different genres, Orgill, a music veteran and critic, offers her top ten picks of female vocalists. She illuminates the personal and professional struggles of Sophie Tucker, Ma Rainey, Bessie Smith, Ethel Merman, Judy Garland, Anita O'Day, Joan Baez, Bette

Midler, Madonna, and Lucinda Williams, selecting these women based on their interesting lives, loves, and musical talents. The text includes a discography, bibliography, and index. CWJ

5.37   Philip, Neil, editor. **A Braid of Lives: Native American Child-hood.** Clarion, 2000. ISBN 0-395-64528-X. 96 pp. Intermediate–Middle school. Nonfiction, Ethnic specific.

In *A Braid of Lives*, Philip weaves together the memories of Native American childhoods. The vignettes are taken from the oral accounts of individuals from over twenty different tribes. Historical photographs accompany the vignettes. Although it is not readily apparent, the book is organized by themes, ranging from children's games to spiritual quests. Teachers may need to help students use the book, perhaps by linking the vignettes with other texts or reading portions aloud. (Informative and Educational Books; Visibility) LCJ

5.38   Philip, Neil. **The Great Mystery: Myths of Native America.** Clarion, 2001. ISBN 0-395-98405-X. 145 pp. Middle school. Myth/folklore, Cross-cultural.

In his introduction, Philip tells us, "A myth is a special kind of story—not simply entertainment but a record of sacred events and a basis for ritual and belief." Each of the chapters in this book presents myths of the indigenous groups of various North American geographic areas. The myths are woven together in a way that helps the reader understand the relationships between different myths, but also to glimpse the individual character of tribes and even storytellers. Photographs accompany the text. TLC

5.39   Ray, Deborah Kogan. **Hokusai: The Man Who Painted a Mountain.** Illustrated by Deborah Kogan Ray. Farrar, Straus and Giroux, 2001. ISBN 0-374-33263-0. Unpaged. Primary–Intermediate. Biography, World.

This is a story about Hokusai Katsushika, one of the greatest artists Japan ever produced. The book describes his life and his passion for drawing, and contains some reproductions of his drawings, including *The Great Wave Off Kanagawa*. The chronology, bibliography, and biographical notes make it possible for students to put Hokusai's life into historical perspective. This text will help students become more familiar with old Japanese society and its customs. IL

5.40 Ringgold, Faith. **Cassie's Colorful Day.** Illustrated by Faith Ringgold. Crown, 1999. ISBN 0-517-80021-7. Unpaged. Primary. Fiction.

In this companion book to *Counting to Tar Beach,* Cassie takes readers through the primary colors as she prepares for an outing to the ice cream parlor with her father. Not all of the colors will meet young children's expectations for primary colors. NHK

5.41 Sonneborn, Liz. **The New York Public Library Amazing Native American History: A Book of Answers for Kids.** Wiley, 1999. ISBN 0-471-33204-6. 170 pp. Intermediate–Middle school. Nonfiction.

This text provides information on several North American native cultures. Organized by regional group (from Mesoamerica to subarctic and arctic regions), with attention to tribal groups and a chapter titled "Native Americans Today," each chapter takes a historical approach and is written in question-and-answer format. The book includes some photographs and reproductions, a glossary, a bibliography, and a suggested reading list. Because of the wide range covered, topics are given surface-level treatment. Students might best use this book as a beginning resource. TLC

5.42 Stanley, Jerry. **Hurry Freedom: African Americans in Gold Rush California.** Crown, 2000. ISBN 0-517-80094-2. 86 pp. Intermediate–Middle school. Nonfiction, Cross-cultural.

Award-winning nonfiction writer Jerry Stanley recounts the history of African Americans during the California gold rush of 1849, capturing this historical period through the true accounts of Mifflin Wistar Gibbs and Peter Lester. The possibility of greater freedom and wealth on the West Coast lure both Gibbs and Lester. Unfortunately, they, like other African Americans, find the same injustices and racist attitudes in California. Ultimately, both men prosper, assist in the Underground Railroad, and lead the California community in obtaining equal rights by overturning the laws prohibiting African Americans from testifying in California courts. End pieces provide documentation and resources for further research. (War and Resilience; Social Responsibility) EMA

5.43   Staub, Frank. **Children of the Tlingit.** Photographs by Frank Staub. Carolrhoda, 1999. ISBN 1-57505-333-0. 48 pp. Elementary–Intermediate. Nonfiction, Ethnic specific.

This reference book about the Tlingit tribe of southeastern Alaska includes some history about the migration of the Native Americans, as well as the subsequent Russian and American occupations of the area beginning in the early 1800s. The photographs are primarily of Tlingit children engaging in both traditional and non-native activities. *Children of the Tlingit* is an excellent book for portraying Tlingit culture as it exists today, as well as how the tribe has maintained some important traditions. MBC

5.44   Stolley, Richard B., editor. **LIFE: Our Century in Pictures for Young People.** Little, Brown, 2000. ISBN 0-316-81589-6. 223 pp. Middle school. Nonfiction.

LIFE magazine features snapshots from the worlds of sports, entertainment, politics, art, social activism, science, and technology for younger audiences. The book illuminates events and people that made headlines during the twentieth century. Each chapter contains an essay by a well-known children's writer, a section that highlights key trends that endured throughout the century, and a section that pays homage to a few who died during that era. This work relies heavily on popular media portrayals and individuals who have reached icon status. Some less popular historical gems are unearthed, but many remain unchronicled. CWJ

5.45   Tallchief, Maria, with Rosemary Wells. **Tallchief: America's Prima Ballerina.** Illustrated by Gary Kelley. Viking, 1999. ISBN 0-670-88756-0. 28 pp. Intermediate. Autobiography, Ethnic specific.

"My name is Elizabeth Marie Tallchief. I was born with music that flowed as naturally through my body as blood in my veins. This was a gift from God. I became a pioneer for American dance, and this was a gift from my mother." So begins this autobiography by Maria Tallchief, a prima ballerina who was born on an Osage Indian reservation in Oklahoma. This is an inspirational story about a half Native American woman who, through dedication and talent, became one of the most revered ballerinas of our time. (Visibility) MBC

5.46   Varriale, Jim. **Kids Dance: The Students of Ballet Tech.** Dutton, 1999. ISBN 0-525-45535-1. Unpaged. Intermediate and up. Nonfiction.

This book about the students of America's first public school for ballet provides a glimpse into how the students are chosen, are trained, and eventually perform under the careful tutelage of the expertly trained faculty. The story is told through beautiful photographs and quotes from the students themselves. (Families, Friends, and Community; Visibility) MBC

5.47   Waldman, Neil. **Wounded Knee.** Atheneum, 2001. ISBN 0-689-82559-5. 54 pp. Intermediate–Middle school. Nonfiction, Cross-cultural.

Waldman provides a thought-provoking account of the massacre at Wounded Knee. The text begins with a heart-wrenching description of the battle from the viewpoint of Lakota warrior Black Elk. Subsequent chapters explore the series of cultural clashes that seem to lead inevitably toward violent conflict. This is a balanced perspective on an event to which schoolchildren should be introduced. An epilogue provides information about modern Lakota peoples. The text includes a brief bibliography and index but would benefit from source notes and maps. (War and Resilience) TLC

5.48   Wallace, Mary. **The Inuksuk Book.** Owl, 1999. ISBN 1-895688-90-6. 64 pp. Intermediate. Nonfiction.

This is a great source book for exploring Inuk culture. Inuit are descendants of people who have lived in Arctic North America for over 4,000 years. Using old and recent pictures and illustrations, as well as some Inuktitut words, the author explains the lives and cultures of the Inuit, connecting their traditions to the title, *Inuksuk,* which is a unique stone structure. A guide to building an inuksuk, provided at the end of the book, will give children a chance to connect to this culture through hands-on experience. (Families, Friends, and Community; Visibility) IL

5.49 Weatherford, Carole Boston. **The Sound That Jazz Makes.** Illustrated by Eric Velasquez. Walker, 2000. ISBN 0-8027-8720-7. Unpaged. All ages. Nonfiction.

This beautifully illustrated and brief look into the influences of jazz music provides snapshots of African American and music history. The text makes huge leaps with little contextual information, thereby whetting the reader's appetite for opportunities to make more significant connections between African American legacies and jazz music. All readers will benefit from looking more deeply into the historical dimensions outlined in this work. Historical explanations and recommendations for further reading would have strengthened this book. CWJ

5.50 Winter, Jonah. **Fair Ball! 14 Great Stars from Baseball's Negro Leagues.** Illustrated by Jonah Winter. Scholastic, 1999. ISBN 0-590-39464-9. Unpaged. Elementary–Intermediate. Biography, Ethnic specific.

"Everyone has heard of Babe Ruth, Lou Gehrig, and Ty Cobb.... But how many people have heard of Pop Lloyd, Oscar Charleston, or Buck Leonard?" Through beautiful illustrations and brief but informative biographies, the reader is treated to a concise history of the greats who played in the Negro Baseball Leagues. By highlighting the amazing talent and stories of a group of athletes who have been all but ignored, Winter provides an invaluable addition to any classroom's biography collection. (Visibility) MBC

5.51 Wormser, Richard. **The Rise & Fall of Jim Crow: The African-American Struggle Against Discrimination, 1865–1954.** Franklin Watts, 1999. ISBN 0-531-11443-0. 144 pp. Intermediate–Middle school. Nonfiction.

This excellent resource documents the historical development and legacy of segregation under Jim Crow laws in the United States. First-person narratives, illustrations, and contemporary documents take the reader on the journey that our country has taken as it dealt with race relations and policy. The text highlights the endurance that African Americans have needed throughout the decades to gain their civil rights. By creatively linking the past to the present, from Reconstruction to the 1954 Supreme Court decision and beyond, the authors introduce readers to the events that shaped U.S. history and contemporary struggles. (War and Resilience; Social Responsibility) MVW

5.52 Yue, Charlotte, and David Yue. **The Wigwam and the Longhouse.** Houghton Mifflin, 2000. ISBN 0-395-84169-0. 112 pp. Intermediate–Middle school. Nonfiction.

Although the focus of this text is on the traditional houses of Native Americans from the northeastern United States, the Yues provide far more. The authors situate their descriptions of wigwam and longhouse construction in the historical period, environment, lifestyle, and culture of the people who built them. Chapters toward the end of the book address the clash of cultures that occurred when White settlers arrived, as well as a very brief glimpse into Native American life today. The text is greatly enhanced by the numerous and detailed drawings. TLC

6 Visibility

Mary Beth Canty and Incho Lee

When I was in grade school, I was taunted and bullied because of my Korean heritage. I was frequently asked, "What are you, a Chink or a Jap?" I can still remember the embarrassment I felt when I saw books such as *The Seven Chinese Brothers.* The brothers' exaggerated slanted eyes and big round cheeks made me wonder how anyone could believe that those illustrations were an accurate portrayal of anyone of Asian descent. I quickly learned the power that literature has in shaping and molding young, impressionable minds.

It wasn't until I was a graduate student at the University of Washington that I was first introduced to ethnic-specific literature. The idea that people of color, not just kids who looked like Sally, Dick and Jane, also had the right to respect, visibility, and kept promises (Hansen-Krening, 1997) was a startling revelation to me. Up to that point, I had never seen myself in picture books, nor did I identify with any particular character's experience

—Mary Beth Canty, 2002

As Hansen-Krening (1997) states, "All children have the right to see themselves mirrored in literature in a sensitive and accurate portrayal." The books in this chapter on visibility range from positive portrayals of people of various ethnicities, to culturally neutral depictions, to inaccurate stereotypes. According to Bishop (1993), the term *culturally neutral* means that the books "feature people of color, but are fundamentally about something else" (p. 46). The story and/or pictures could be of anyone from any ethnic background; the ethnic identity is unimportant to either the story line or the reader's understanding of the characters. This type of book has both positive and negative ramifications.

Culturally neutral literature in the classroom does not introduce students to specific ethnic and cultural traditions. A book that shows Asian Americans, for example, in its illustrations but doesn't address any issues of cultural heritage would not be an appropriate choice for helping children better understand life as a Japanese American. Keats's stories about Peter, such as *The Snowy Day* (1962), are delightful to read and look at but certainly don't expose the reader to the culturally determined experiences of an African American child. These neutral portrayals enable virtually any reader to place himself or herself into the story because there is an absence of any ethnic-specific language or experience.

Although some of the books listed in this chapter are culturally neutral, many of them are not. The latter accurately reflect the diversity of races and ethnicities found within U.S. society. The books also show the richness and complexity within ethnicities. In *Turtle Island* (Curry, 1999), for instance, the stories are told in the oral tradition of the Algonquian nation. Here is a prime example of an ethnic group, Algonquian Indians, that is frequently lumped together with tribes from all over North America. In fact, each nation has varied and different traditions that are distinct from one another. The idea that all folks in any one group look, act, or are the same is negated in books such as these.

The books in this chapter also highlight the dilemma now faced by many of us who are struggling to understand the events of September 11, 2001. How does one retain his or her ethnic and cultural identity, traditions, and culture but still be considered an "American"? The urgency to help dispel negative stereotypes of Muslims, Arab Americans, and people of other Middle East cultures is a pressing issue in many schools around the country. Just as these people need to identify as Americans, the need to appreciate their rich heritages is equally pressing. We are reminded of a recent picture in the newspaper of a mosque in Oregon, encircled and protected by a chain of very "white"-looking folks holding a sign that read, "Pray in peace. We will guard you." For many Muslims and Arab Americans, the message that they too are American has become a matter of life and death.

There is, then, a continuum on the scale of visibility. At one end are those books portraying themes, topics, values, and attitudes of a specific ethnic group in a way that invokes stereotypical characteristics to imply or connote ethnicity. Doing so often negates the purpose the author or illustrator might have intended. For those of us whose ethnic identities have been misunderstood or maligned, these books do nothing to help dispel misinformation, and we have not included books from this end of the visibility scale. It is critical to remember that the United States of America is a country whose citizens are proud not only of being "American," but also of their ethnic and cultural heritages. We want to preserve our ethnic and cultural heritages but not be defined solely by them. In the middle of the continuum are fine books that show all of us visibly leading everyday contemporary lives. In these stories, our ethnic identity is perceptible in today's society, yet ethnic membership does not drive the story. This type of portrayal helps underscore the importance of the many things we have in common, not just our country of residence. At the other end of the continuum are those books that reveal the complexity of our ethnic heritages in authentic, realistic ways that help others understand who we are, where we come from, and our similarities to and differences from peoples of different backgrounds. These books promote tolerance of diversity and acceptance of the principle that the American character is derived from a multiplicity of ideas and voices, not from conformity.

> Responsibility is what gives a person worth and dignity. Responsibility is a value meaning to be responsible for a life or even knowing that every action has a reaction. If you become responsible for your actions, you will change a whole lot. You will think before you do things. So many people don't hold themselves responsible for things.
>
> —Antonio, in Allison (1999), p. 167

References

Allison, A. (1999). *Hear these voices: Youth at the edge of the millennium*. New York: Dutton.

Bishop, R. S. (1993). Multicultural literature for children: Making informed choices. In V. J. Harris (Ed.), *Teaching multicultural literature in grades K–8* (pp. 37–53). Norwood, MA: Christopher-Gordon.

Hansen-Krening, N. (1997). Unpublished lecture notes, Education: Curriculum and Instruction 505, Ethnic Specific Literature in the Classroom. Seattle: University of Washington.

6.1 Allen, Debbie. **Dancing in the Wings.** Illustrated by Kadir Nelson. Dial, 2000. ISBN 0-8037-2501-9. Unpaged. Primary–Intermediate. Fiction, Ethnic specific.

"My mom calls me Sassy, 'cause I like to put my hands on my hips and 'cause I always have something to say. Well, if you had feet as big as mine, you'd understand why." It may be just that attitude that helps Sassy persevere in her dream of being a ballerina. This is a charming twenty-first century version of the ugly-duckling-becoming-the-elegant-swan story. (Families, Friends, and Community) NHK

6.2   Alvarez, Julia. **The Secret Footprints.** Illustrated by Fabian Negrin. Knopf, 2000. ISBN 0-679-89309-6. Unpaged. All ages. Myth/folklore, World.

How fortunate that Julia Alvarez has made that difficult transition from adult literature to children's literature. She has done so with style in her fascinating version of a traditional folktale from the Dominican Republic about a magical girl whose ocean people, the *ciguapa,* all have their feet on backwards. The young girl, Guapa, loves delicious land food so intensely that she is almost captured by land people. (Families, Friends, and Community) NHK

6.3   Arcellana, Francisco. **The Mats.** Illustrated by Hermès Alègrè. Kane/Miller, 1999. ISBN 0-916291-86-3. Unpaged. Primary. Fiction.

An adult student from the Philippines was moved to tears when she saw this book included in one of her classes in the United States. The author and illustrator are well-known and well-loved artists in her country but have not achieved equal fame here. The warmth of family love and remembrance in this lovely and simple story will endear both artists to adults and children alike. All readers can respond to the story of Papa returning from a long trip with gifts for each member of the family—even for those who are no longer present. NHK

6.4   Bruchac, Joseph, and James Bruchac, retellers. **How Chipmunk Got His Stripes: A Tale of Bragging and Teasing.** Illustrated by Jose Aruego and Ariane Dewey. Dial, 2001. ISBN 0-8037-2402-7. Unpaged. Primary. Myth/folklore, Ethnic specific.

Father and son storytellers Joseph and James Bruchac collaborate in this retelling of a Native American *pourquoi* tale of how the chipmunk got his stripes. In their authors' note, the team traces the origins of this story to its Cherokee, Abenaki, Mohawk, and Iroquois sources. This traditional tale of the challenge and quarrel between Big Bear and Brown Squirrel to stop the sun from rising ultimately teaches young readers about anger and pride. This story is vividly illustrated by the team of Jose Aruego and Ariane Dewey. EMA

6.5   Choi, Yangsook. **New Cat.** Illustrated by Yangsook Choi. Francis Foster Books, 1999. ISBN 0-374-35512-6. Unpaged. Primary. Fiction, Ethnic specific.

New Cat, living in Mr. Kim's tofu factory, is his best friend and saves the factory from burning down by spilling tofu over an electrical wire that has caught fire. Although the author provides at the end of the book a brief description of her own experiences of eating and cooking tofu in Korea, and though the author herself, like Mr. Kim, is Korean American, the story is not necessarily about Korean or Korean American culture, because the main message of this book would not change if the tofu factory were replaced by an Italian American spaghetti factory. (Families, Friends, and Community) IL

6.6   Collier, Bryan. **Uptown.** Illustrated by Bryan Collier. Henry Holt, 2000. ISBN 0-8050-5721-8. Unpaged. Primary. Nonfiction, Ethnic specific.

The young narrator allows us to participate with him in a glorious celebration of today's Harlem. We see and feel the community of the Harlem Boy's Choir, the community of shared landmarks, and the community of safety and home. All readers need to experience this alternative perspective on the media myth of Harlem. (Families, Friends, and Community) NHK

6.7   Curry, Jane Louise. **Turtle Island: Tales of the Algonquian Nations.** Illustrated by James Watts. Margaret K. McElderry Books, 1999. ISBN 0-689-82233-2. 145 pp. Intermediate. Myth/folklore, Cross-cultural.

The author clearly states that the stories in this collection of Algonquian Indian tales are her versions told in her own words. What she has created is a collection of folklore that draws from different tribes within the Algonquian Nation. Readers will find her versions short and interesting. (Families, Friends, and Community) NHK

6.8   Falwell, Cathryn. **David's Drawings.** Illustrated by Cathryn Falwell. Lee & Low, 2001. ISBN 1-58430-031-0. Unpaged. Primary. Fiction.

David creates a drawing of a tree at school. Some classmates take an interest and add their own touches. Along the way, David makes some friends. This is a sweet story about finding activities that can help people reach out and help build bridges between friends. (Families, Friends, and Community) MBC

6.9   Gelman, Rita Golden. **Rice Is Life.** Illustrated by Yangsook Choi. Henry Holt, 2000. ISBN 0-8050-5719-6. Unpaged. Primary–Intermediate. Fiction, World.

Rice is the essence of life in Bali, Indonesia; a traditional Balinese family eats rice for breakfast, lunch, and dinner. In this beautifully presented book, Gelmen examines the relationship between the spiritual and material world by portraying the significance of rice to the people of Bali. Through the integration of poetry and information, enhanced by Choi's exquisite illustrations, the daily experience of life in Bali is brought to life. (Informative and Educational Books) DH & DB

6.10   Gilchrist, Cherry, reteller. **Stories from the Silk Road.** Illustrated by Nilesh Mistry. Barefoot, 1999. ISBN 1-902283-25-2. 79 pp. Intermediate. Myth/folklore, World.

By actually tracing the route of the Silk Road, author and illustrator present vivid versions of folktales found in different geographical locations. The book is a clever combination of nonfiction information about the historical route and the value of silk and folktales, and lends itself well to read-alouds. (War and Resilience; Families, Friends, and Community) NHK

6.11   Havill, Juanita. **Jamaica and the Substitute Teacher.** Illustrated by Anne Sibley O'Brien. Houghton Mifflin, 1999. ISBN 0-395-90503-6. Unpaged. Primary. Fiction.

A substitute teacher enters the classroom, and Jamaica does her best to impress this creative educator. Jamaica does very well in reading, finding hidden objects, and solving math problems and earns many positive comments from the substitute teacher. But Jamaica forgets about a spelling test and doesn't remember how to spell *calf*. Havill once again presents us with a Jamaica story and how she resolves a moral dilemma. This sensitive story takes place within a diverse classroom setting. EMA

6.12   Hoffman, Mary. **Starring Grace.** Illustrated by Caroline Binch. Phyllis Fogelman Books, 2000. ISBN 0-8037-2559-0. 95 pp. Intermediate. Fiction, World.

Grace is back. It's summer and Grace and her friends are ready for new adventures. In their make-believe world, they become everything from doctors to astronauts. In the real world, they have an opportunity to turn their talents for pretend into an exciting onstage experience. Grace's fans will not be disappointed. (Families, Friends, and Community) TLC

6.13 Hofmeyr, Dianne. **The Star-Bearer.** Illustrated by Jude Daly. Farrar, Straus and Giroux, 2001. ISBN 0-374-37181-4. Unpaged. Intermediate. Myth/folklore, World.

The illustrations of this version of an Egyptian creation myth are stunning in their beauty. The text is a bit difficult to follow. NHK

6.14 Hurst, Margaret M. **Grannie and the Jumbie: A Caribbean Tale.** Illustrated by Margaret M. Hurst. HarperCollins, 2001. ISBN 0-06-623632-0. Unpaged. Preschool–Primary. Myth/folklore, World.

This Caribbean folktale is written in authentic rhythmic language. Emanuel thinks his granny is superstitious but eventually realizes that she is wise and finds himself listening to her after evil Jumbie's visit. The illustrations are quite distinctive, incorporating colorful fabrics from the author's native St. Thomas. A glossary is provided. IL

6.15 Ichikawa, Satomi. **The First Bear in Africa!** Philomel, 2001. ISBN 0-399-23485-3. Unpaged. Primary. Fiction, World.

This simple, charming story is told through the perspective of young Meto, who lives with his family in the middle of the African savanna. One day Meto and his family show some tourists the savanna animals. When the family of tourists leaves, Meto realizes that the small animal the little girl had been holding is a teddy bear, which she has dropped. Meto takes a shortcut and, with the help of his animal friends, returns the lost teddy bear. This small tale is a good introduction to the African savanna, its animals, and Swahili words for very young readers. EMA

6.16 Krishnaswami, Uma, reteller. **Shower of Gold: Girls and Women in the Stories of India.** Illustrated by Maniam Selven. Linnet, 1999. ISBN 0-208-02484-0. 125 pp. Intermediate–Middle school. Myth/folklore, World.

If you want a beautifully written collection of folktales featuring women and girls from India, this is your book. If you want a book whose accuracy you can trust, this is your book. Readers are often on shaky ground when choosing folktales and myths from other cultures. How certain can one be that these versions are respected and accepted by the culture of origin? Here, the collection has a ring of authenticity when the author states explicitly that she (or he) is providing the versions she knows and that she cannot represent all women and girls in India. NHK

6.17   McDermott, Gerald, reteller. **Raven: A Trickster Tale from the Pacific Northwest.** Illustrated by Gerald McDermott. Voyager, 2001. ISBN 0-15-202449-2. Unpaged. Preschool–Primary. Myth/ folklore, Cross-cultural.

This is a traditional Native American folktale of the bird Raven who brought light to people after journeying to find the sun. The author's note about how to make a totem pole and magical boxes seems to disregard the true nature of totem poles. The accuracy of McDermott's works has been questioned (see *Through Indian Eyes: The Native Experience in Books for Children* [Slapin & Seale, 1998]), so teachers are encouraged to consult reviews by Native Americans before using McDermott's books. IL

6.18   Nikola-Lisa, W. **Can You Top That?** Illustrated by Hector Viveros Lee. Lee & Low, 2000. ISBN 1-880000-99-7. Unpaged. Primary. Fiction, Cross-cultural.

"I got a horse with ten heads! Can you top that?" In this beautifully illustrated book, Nikola-Lisa is able to integrate the counting of wacky animals, from one fish with one fin to a horse with ten heads, with a narrative that stimulates and encourages children's imaginations. Friends at the park draw animals on the ground in a competition to see which has the most impressive animal—until one boy offers a simple and surprising challenge. DH & DB

6.19   Nikola-Lisa, W. **Hallelujah! A Christmas Celebration.** Illustrated by Synthia Saint James. Atheneum, 2000. ISBN 0-689-81673-1. Unpaged. Preschool–Primary. Fiction, Cross-cultural.

This is the well-known story of a newborn Jesus; the only difference is that he has dark skin. Creative, simplified illustrations in vibrant color create an atmosphere of mystery. This book will give younger readers a valuable opportunity to start mulling over false or dubious tenets of what might be considered common knowledge. IL

6.20   Ringgold, Faith. **Counting to Tar Beach.** Illustrated by Faith Ringgold. Crown, 1999. ISBN 0-517-80022-5. Unpaged. Primary. Fiction, Ethnic specific.

Faith Ringgold has taken her beautiful quilt art and story line from the famous *Tar Beach* and turned them into a charming counting board book. She begins the story by counting one watermelon, two baskets of chicken, and so on to the last page, where she asks young readers to count the number of things Cassie took to the picnic on Tar Beach—and then to count the stars in the sky where Cassie flies. This is an excellent and durable resource for primary grade teachers. (Families, Friends, and Community) NHK

6.21   Rochelle, Belinda, compiler. **Words with Wings: A Treasury of African-American Poetry and Art.** HarperCollins, 2001. ISBN 0-688-16415-3. Unpaged. Middle school and up. Fiction, Ethnic specific.

A breathtaking sampling of the works of African American poets and artists makes up this unique anthology of poetry. Rochelle has put together an inspirational and powerful book of poetry and art that explores the African American experience both today and throughout history. (War and Resilience; Friends, Families, and Community) MBC

6.22   Schwartz, Howard, and Barbara Rush, compilers and retellers. **A Coat for the Moon and Other Jewish Tales.** Illustrated by Michael Iofin. Jewish Publication Society, 1999. ISBN 0-8276-0596-X. 81 pp. Intermediate–Middle school. Myth/folklore, World.

Teachers could use this collection of Jewish folktales from around the world to help students consider alternative endings for the stories. "The Witch Barusha," for example, the story of a father who wants to save his children from a witch, could be substituted with a father who wants to save not only his own children but also *all* children. IL

6.23   Siddals, Mary McKenna. **I'll Play with You.** Illustrated by David Wisniewski. Clarion, 2000. ISBN 0-395-90373-4. 28 pp. Preschool. Fiction.

I'll Play with You is about a child's everyday life—playing with the sun, wind, and clouds. Many children will recognize themselves in this story because the illustrations include children from diverse ethnic backgrounds. IL

6.24   Sierra, Judy. **The Gift of the Crocodile: A Cinderella Story.** Illustrated by Reynold Ruffins. Simon & Schuster, 2000. ISBN 0-689-82188-3. Unpaged. Primary. Myth/folklore, World.

This Cinderella tale comes from the island of Halmahera in the Moluccas, or Spice Islands, in Indonesia. In this version, instead of a fairy godmother, it is a grandmother crocodile who recognizes Damura's kind heart and assists the girl using her magical powers. Damura meets her prince, loses her slipper, and finally marries the prince. Her stepsister and mother, however, continue their wicked practices until finally they are driven into the darkest part of the forest. Sierra's straightforward retelling helps readers find the universal elements in the story, while Ruffin's bright motif paintings add tropical folk flavors to this familiar tale. EMA

6.25   Smith, Charles R. Jr. **Loki and Alex: The Adventures of a Dog and His Best Friend.** Illustrated by Charles R. Smith Jr. Dutton, 2001. ISBN 0-525-46700-9. Unpaged. Intermediate. Nonfiction.

This delightful book about Alex, a young African American boy, and Loki, his dog and best friend, is jointly narrated by Alex and Loki. Color photos depict Alex's point of view and black-and-white photos illustrate Loki's. This is a touching story about a boy and his best friend. (Families, Friends, and Community) MBC

6.26   Weatherspoon, Teresa, with Tara Sullivan and Kelly Whiteside. **Teresa Weatherspoon's Basketball for Girls.** Wiley, 1999. ISBN 0-471-31784-5. 120 pp. Intermediate–Middle school. Nonfiction.

Olympic and WNBA professional basketball star Teresa Weatherspoon shares detailed information about the techniques and strategies of her sport. Interspersed throughout the text are photos to highlight the print details. Weatherspoon also shares her personal history and provides inspirational words of advice. EMA

6.27   Wong, Janet S. **Buzz.** Illustrated by Margaret Chodos-Irvine. Harcourt, 2000. ISBN 0-15-201923-5. Unpaged. Primary. Fiction, Ethnic specific.

Buzz is a sweet story about a child's busy morning. Delightful illustrations and simple yet engaging text make this a modern-day story about a young child whose parents both work. Grandma comes to take care of him while Mom and Dad are at work. The morning routine is interrupted by a variety of things that go buzz. MBC

6.28   Wong, Janet S. **This Next New Year.** Illustrated by Yangsook Choi. Farrar, Straus and Giroux, 2000. ISBN 0-374-35503-7. Unpaged. Primary. Fiction, Ethnic specific and Cross-cultural.

Wong has published mostly poetry for older children. Now she has written a wonderful narrative story for youngsters. The perspective is that of a little boy who lives in a multiethnic, multicultural world in which traditions surrounding the New Year are shared by one and all. The boy is determined to do everything he can to make the New Year happy and lucky. Choi uses strong colors and stylized illustrations to draw us into the little boy's world. (Families, Friends, and Community) NHK

6.29   Yep, Laurence. **Cockroach Cooties.** Hyperion, 2000. ISBN 0-786-80487-4. 135 pp. Intermediate. Fiction, Ethnic specific.

This is the second story about brothers Bobby and Teddy and their ongoing struggles with bullies, family, and relationships. Lest that sound too serious, these are stories that entertain with good humor and shared laughter. Teddy continues to do his best to figure all of the angles, while little brother Bobby continues with his ingenuous and honest approach to daily conflicts and problems. This particular book represents visibility simply because the ethnic membership of its characters is clear, but ethnicity stays in the background of the story and emerges as naturally as it does in daily life. The story is a terrific read-aloud for an entire class. (Families, Friends, and Community) NHK

Author Index

Illustrator Index

Subject Index

Title Index

Editors

Elaine M. Aoki received her Ph.D. from the University of Washington. She is currently an elementary principal at the Bush School in Seattle. She has also been a district K–12 reading/language arts coordinator and classroom teacher. Her interests in literacy instruction include children's literature, comprehension, and response to literature. She has been on the authorship team of Macmillan/McGraw Hill's K–8 New View reading series and A New View language arts series, and she also has been a contributing author on professional books about multicultural literature. She coauthored the children's book *The White Swan Express: A Story about Adoption* (2002). Recently Aoki was appointed by the governor to Washington State's Professional Educator Standards Board. She has won numerous educational awards including Washington State's Award for Excellence in Education and the University of Washington's Distinguished Graduate Award.

Nancy Hansen-Krening received her Ph.D. in 1974 and joined the literacy, language, and culture faculty of the University of Washington's College of Education, where she is also an affiliate professor at the Center for Multicultural Education. She served as a foreign expert for two years in the People's Republic of China, where she taught academic English to university professors and graduate students. Hansen-Krening has published two books, authored and coauthored chapters for edited publications and articles, and regularly offered inservice teacher workshops and institutes on children's literature and ethnic-specific literature.

Donald T. Mizokawa was born in "Hell's Half Acre" in downtown Honolulu, the first area of the city to undergo "urban renewal." Trained as a secondary English teacher, he eventually earned a Ph.D. from Indiana University in educational psychology with a strong interest in psycholinguistics and language learning. He is currently professor of educational psychology at the University of Washington.

Contributors

R. Debbie Bier, born in Santiago, Chile, holds a certificate in Montessori education and a master's in education, curriculum, and instruction from Seattle University. She has been a successful educator for many years in Montessori schools, teaching children ages two and a half to twelve, and in the Bellevue School District, Bellevue, Washington, teaching in the Spanish Immersion Program. She participates in the Developing Mathematical Ideas (DMI) program at the University of Washington and is a math leader in her school district. Being multilingual herself, Bier is a strong advocate of multilingual education.

Mary Beth Canty received her Master of Education at the University of Washington and is currently an elementary school teacher at an independent school in Seattle. She feels passionately about the importance of exposing children to ethnic-specific literature and looks forward to the day when ethnic-specific literature is in such abundance that it will no longer be considered a subcategory.

Tracy L. Coskie is a former middle school language arts teacher also certified as a reading specialist. She is currently a Ph.D. student at the University of Washington in curriculum and instruction, specializing in language, literacy, and culture. Her research interests include the literacy-identity relationship, peer-led literature discussions, and content area literacy.

Deborah Hinton, a native of San Juan, Puerto Rico, is a second-grade teacher in a Spanish-immersion program in the Bellevue School District in Washington and a leading advocate of programs encouraging multicultural and multilingual understanding. She has a degree in Spanish and French from the University of South Florida and has taught foreign languages for twenty-two years.

Carolyn W. Jackson is a Ph.D. candidate in curriculum and instruction at the University of Washington. Her areas of study and research interests include multicultural education, ethnic-specific literature, women's studies, and sociocultural foundations of education. She also has undertaken an array of leadership roles associated with college-level recruitment and retention of students of color. Jackson is currently working with a team of authors on a book about their journeys toward becoming multicultural educators. In addition, she is part of the Expanding the Community of Mathematics Learners (ECML) research project, funded by an NSF grant. Her dissertation research will explore the educational careers and ethnic-identity development of former military dependents.

Laura C. Jones is assistant professor of education at Nazareth College of Rochester in New York. She teaches Pre-K–12 literacy education courses to both undergraduate and graduate students.

Kipchoge Kirkland received his doctorate in curriculum and instruction, with a specialization in multicultural education, from the University of Washington and is currently assistant professor of curriculum and instruction at Indiana University. His research and teaching interests include multicultural education, ethnic-specific literature in research and the classroom, African American cultural identity among high school students, urban education, social studies and civic education, and using the arts in teaching and learning to help students develop critical cultural consciousness. His publications include a joint journal article and several chapters in books.

Incho Lee was born in Seoul, Korea and is currently a Ph.D. candidate in curriculum and instruction, specializing in English as a Second Language, at the University of Washington. Her research interests include multicultural literature, ideological aspects of the English language, and language attitudes. Her latest project explores the relationships between globalization and the English language in Korea.

Jerry Purcell has worked as staff at the University of Washington since 1981. He was originally trained in secondary education and was one of the first male Head Start teachers in Washington State. He has worked as a teacher in a program for high school dropouts and illiterate adults, was program manager of a local antipoverty program, and was a K–12 tutor for Native American students.

Michelle VanderVelde Woodfork is lecturer in the Woodring College of Education at Western Washington University. Her primary area of research is the role of the principal as an advocate and leader of multicultural education at the school and district levels. She also conducts professional development for public and private educational organizations on teacher leadership for equity and diversity, ethnic-specific children's literature, and understanding multicultural education. VanderVelde Woodfork received the Phi Delta Kappan International Graduate Scholarship in 2000 and the University Council of Educational Administration Richard L. Clark National Fellowship in 2001.

This book was typeset in Palatino and Helvetica by Precision Graphics.
Typefaces used on the cover were University Roman BT and Book Antiqua.
The book was printed on 50-lb. Husky Offset paper by IPC Communications.